CARIBBEAN PIRATES

BOOKS BY GEORGE BEAHM

The Vaughn Bode Index *(Heresy Press, 1975)*

Kirk's Works: The Art of Tim Kirk *(Heresy Press, 1977)*

How to Sell Woodstoves *(George Beahm, Publisher, 1980)*

How to Buy a Woodstove—and Not Get Burned
(George Beahm, Publisher, 1980)

Notes from Elam *(GB Publishing, 1983)*

The Great Taste of Virginia Seafood *(GB Publishing, 1984)*

How to Publish and Sell Your Cookbook:
A Guide for Fundraisers *(GB Publishing, 1985)*

Write to the Top: How to Complain and Get Results—Fast!
(The Donning Company, 1988)

The Stephen King Companion *(Andrews McMeel Publishing, 1989)*

The Stephen King Story *(Andrews McMeel Publishing, 1990)*

War of Words: The Censorship Debate
(Andrews McMeel Publishing, 1993)

Michael Jordan: Shooting Star *(Andrews McMeel Publishing, 1994)*

The Stephen King Companion
(revised and expanded, Andrews McMeel Publishing, 1995)

The Unauthorized Anne Rice Companion
(Andrews McMeel Publishing, 1995)

Stephen King: America's Best-Loved Boogeyman
(Andrews McMeel Publishing, 1998)

Stephen King from A to Z *(Andrews McMeel Publishing, 1998)*

Stephen King Country *(Running Press, 1999)*

Stephen King Collectibles *(Betts Books, 2000)*

The Patricia Cornwell Companion *(St. Martin's Press, 2002)*

The Essential J. R. R. Tolkien Sourcebook *(New Page Books, 2003)*

How to Protect Yourself and Your Family against Terrorism
(Potomac Books, 2003)

Muggles and Magic: An Unofficial Guide to J. K. Rowling and the Harry
Potter Phenomenon *(Hampton Roads Publishing, 2004)*

Fact, Fiction, and Folklore in Harry Potter's World:
An Unofficial Guide *(Hampton Roads Publishing, 2005)*

Passport to Narnia: A Newcomer's Guide
(Hampton Roads Publishing, 2005)

The Whimsic Alley Book of Spells
(with Stanley Goldin, Hampton Roads Publishing, 2007)

Muggles and Magic: An Unofficial Guide, 3rd Edition
(revised and expanded, Hampton Roads Publishing, 2007)

Stephen King Collectibles *(2nd ed., revised and expanded, Betts Books, 2007)*

Philip Pullman's Dark Materials:
The Golden Compass and Other Stories
(Hampton Roads Publishing, 2007)

Author George Beahm in front of a life-size pirate book on display at an exhibit, "Swashbuckler: Romance of the Pirate," at the Mariners' Museum, Newport News, Virginia.

One of a trio of pirate musicians playing outside the Pirates of the Caribbean ride at New Orleans Square, Disneyland Park, Anaheim, California.

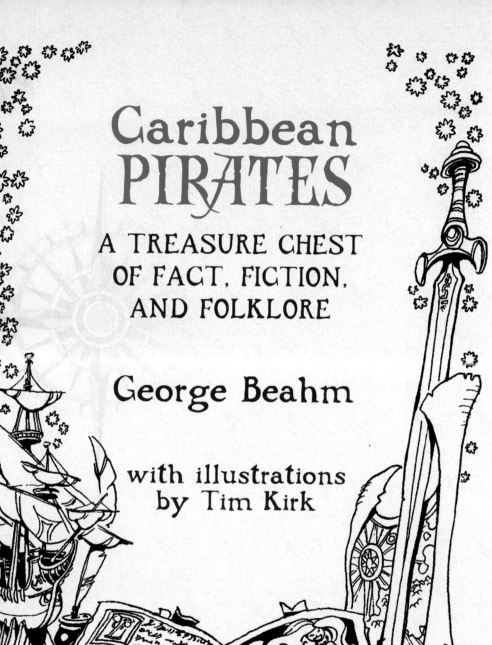

Caribbean PIRATES

A TREASURE CHEST OF FACT, FICTION, AND FOLKLORE

George Beahm

with illustrations
by Tim Kirk

HR
for the evolving human spirit

HAMPTON ROADS
PUBLISHING COMPANY, INC.

Cover Design by Jane Hagaman
Treasure Chest © 2007 by Tim Kirk
1655 Pirate Themed Chart of the Caribbean © 2006 by Jonathan White
Text Design by Steve Amarillo

Hampton Roads Publishing Company, Inc.
1125 Stoney Ridge Road
Charlottesville, VA 22902
434-296-2772
fax: 434-296-5096
e-mail: hrpc@hrpub.com
www.hrpub.com

If you are unable to order this book from your local bookseller,
you may order directly from the publisher. Call 1-800-766-8009.

Library of Congress Cataloging-in-Publication Data

Beahm, George W.
   Caribbean pirates : a treasure chest of fact, fiction, and folklore / George Beahm ; with art by Tim
Kirk. -- 1st ed.
      p. cm.
   Summary: "Drawing from key people, places, and things seen in the Pirates of the Caribbean movies,
author George Beahm gives readers a unique and entertaining look at the rise of the pirate craze and sep-
arates pirate fact from fiction. Caribbean Pirates features a reader-friendly format, covering all aspects of
pirate life and the folklore surrounding the notorious mariners"--Provided by publisher.
   Includes index.
   ISBN 978-1-57174-541-5 (6 x 9 tp : alk. paper)
   1. Pirates--Caribbean Area--Miscellanea. 2. Buccaneers--Miscellanea. 3. Pirates of the Caribbean,
the curse of the black pearl (Motion picture)--Miscellanea. 4. Pirates of the Caribbean, dead man's chest
(Motion picture)--Miscellanea. I. Title.
   F2161.B33 2007
   910.4'509729--dc22

                                                                          2007001822

            ISBN 978-1-57174-541-5 PB
            ISBN 978-1-57174-553-8 HC

            10 9 8 7 6 5 4 3 2 1
            Printed on acid-free paper in China

For "Long John" Tim Kirk and "Black Dog" Stephen Kirk, thank you for sharing your imaginative worlds with the rest of us

Looking past a replica ship out toward the James River, a view from Jamestown Settlement, Jamestown, Virginia.

A movie poster of *Muppet Treasure Island* on display at the Mariners' Museum.

IT'S BETTER TO BE A PIRATE THAN JOIN THE NAVY.

—STEVE JOBS, APPLE COMPUTER

NO PREY, NO PAY.

—POPULAR PIRATE SLOGAN

TABLE OF CONTENTS

SECTION I: PIRATE FACT AND FICTION

FOR HIS SHIP *Revenge*, THE ARTICLES
OF CAPTAIN JOHN PHILLIPS 13

A statue, King Neptune, Ruler of the Seas, on display in the lobby of the Mariners' Museum.

SECTION II: A PIRATE'S LIFE FOR YOU

A life-size cutout of Blackbeard
with his flag, on display
at the Mariners' Museum.

A replica of the ship *Godspeed,* moored at Jamestown Settlement.

FOREWORD

DREAD PIRATE TIMMY OR YO HO HO AND A BOTTLE OF OVALTINE

Arrrr! Avast, ye yellow-bellied bilge rats!

Return with me to the fabulous fifties of my childhood and the swashbuckling Kirk brothers: "Long John" Timmy and his equally murderous kid brother, "Black Dog" Stephen. We were swaggering, scowling little cutthroats, hook-handed and eye-patched, the scourge of the Spanish Main and Long Beach, California. Our quiet, leafy suburban neighborhood rang with cannon fire, musketry, and the clash of steel. Galleons were seized, towns were sacked, prisoners were taken, and treasures were buried--much to the annoyance of our neighbors and relatives. If we couldn't reach the Caribbean, then East Sixty-fifth Street would do just fine, thank you. It was a veritable reign of nautical terror, and ye may lay to that, me hearties! Aye, even the Royal Navy itself was powerless before us!

One cinematic masterpiece from Walt Disney Productions, *Treasure Island* (1950) starring the inimitable Robert Newton as Long John Silver, changed our young lives forever. To us, Robert Newton *was* Long John, and he was the complete, totally satisfying incarnation of what a pirate should be. We sailed with Jim Hawkins on the *Hispaniola* in search of Captain Flint's cursed treasure. We eluded the traitorous mutineers and befriended the crazed Ben Gunn, shuddered at the sight of the Black Spot, aided Captain Smollett's loyal crew in its defense of the blockhouse, and shared in incalculable riches at the happy ending of Robert Louis Stevenson's ageless tale. We drove our long-suffering parents to the brink of insanity with our shrieking imitations of Silver's parrot: "Pieces of eight! Pieces of eight!" I reinvented myself as old Long John, right down to my painful attempt to emulate the wily rascal's one-leggedness by tying my own leg up behind me with a belt and hobbling around the backyard with a homemade crutch. To help us fully realize our imaginative potential—and get us out of the house—our father built a splendid piratical vessel of plywood, complete with main mast, poop deck, gunports, and ship's wheel.

Better than any tree house, our little ship sailed to the ends of the Earth and back, through myriad perils—typhoons, water spouts, the British, Spanish, French, and Dutch navies, jealous fellow pirates, cannibals, sea serpents, and giant squids. We always returned unscathed, laden with doubloons, gold bullion, diamonds, and other various swag and booty. It was a happy fantasy, one that consumed us until Davy Crockett came along, and we became defenders of the Alamo and Santa Anna's army; then Confederate soldiers; and then invading Martians. But piracy, with its romance and intrigue, was the best. Pirates appear, disappear, and reappear in popular culture, from Long John Silver, to Captain Blood, to Captain Hook, to Captain Jack Sparrow: villainous, heroic, scruffy, savage, and colorful, roaming unfettered, wild, and free, and appealing to the anarchic, lawless core of our nature.

I'd like to thank The Walt Disney Company for *Treasure Island* and its worthy successors, the *Pirates of the Caribbean* movies; and thank you, Dad, for inspiring us to dream.

Tim Kirk
January 2007

Prior to the debut of Kirk Design Inc., Tim and Steve Kirk had long and distinguished careers at Walt Disney Imagineering—twenty-two and twenty-five years, respectively. They were fortunate enough to be involved in several of the most exciting projects the company produced in the seventies (Steve's first assignment was a portion of the Land pavilion at EPCOT Center), eighties, and nineties—including a newly designed Tomorrowland for Walt Disney World's Magic Kingdom, the Disney-MGM Studios (including the Tower of Terror) at Walt Disney World Resort, the Pan Galactic Pizza Port for Tokyo Disneyland, and many more. The crowning achievement of both their careers is undoubtedly Tokyo DisneySea, the second gated park for the Tokyo Disney Resort and, arguably, the most gorgeous theme park in the world. Steve served as senior vice president for that project, with overall creative responsibility, and Tim was senior concept designer.

A view of the James River from a replica
ship moored at Jamestown Settlement.

INTRODUCTION

PIRATING: THE SWEET TRADE

Who hasn't dreamed of setting sail to uncharted places and leaving the modern world behind? Who hasn't longed for the freedom associated with the pirate life? Ever since the golden age of pirates, these colorful men, and more than a few women, sailed the seven seas in search of plunder to capture their booty and our imaginations.

Always popular with the public, pirates are back with a vengeance, riding on a high tide of interest created by Disney's film franchise about pirates of the Caribbean. Johnny Depp's inspired interpretation of Captain Jack Sparrow makes us want to leave our mundane world behind, take control of a ship's helm, and sail off to exotic ports worldwide.

This book is your passport to take a walk on the wild side and learn how to be a pirate. On the assumption that you're a landlubber, this book will help you get up to speed fast. The first section will help you separate pirate fact from pirate fiction. Since you've probably seen the Disney *Pirates of the Caribbean* films, I'll use them as a basis for discussion. I'll describe the films and then tell you what's historically accurate and what's not.

The second section, "A Pirate's Life for You," will immerse you in pirate culture. You'll learn how to speak, dress, and live like a pirate. I'll also tell you how to find your way around a pirate ship, point you toward museums that are worth your time and attention, and tell you a little about the Disney pirate ride and its film franchise. By the end of part two, you should be pretty savvy about the

The Rusty Cutlasses (photo courtesy of Pirates in Paradise in Key West, Florida).

sweet trade, so there is a challenging quiz to test your Pirate IQ, complete with detailed answers.

Section three provides recommended resources for when you're ready to sail off on your own and increase your knowledge of piratical and nautical lore. The appendix lists pirate books, films, general websites, and the biggest pirate resource of them all, a cyberspace place well-known and loved within the pirate community called *No Quarter Given*. Plus some Disney resources you'd never know about unless you took a trip to the Walt Disney World Resort in Orlando, Florida.

Now, scamper up the gangplank and find yourself a berth because it's time to shove off and head out to the ports of call on this Caribbean cruise. Let's go find some pirates!

Williamsburg, Virginia
January 2007

PIRATE FACT AND FICTION

What most people know about pirates should probably be tossed overboard, so let's start fresh. Have you seen a few old pirate movies or been to a Renaissance fair once or twice? Did you read *Treasure Island* or watch Disney's *Pirates of the Caribbean* movies? If so, you know *about* pirates, but you don't *know* pirates.

In this section, you'll get the straight poop about what's in *Pirates of the Caribbean: The Curse of the Black Pearl* and *Pirates of the Caribbean: Dead Man's Chest*—what's historically accurate, and what's not. When referring to the former, I'll use the shorthand *Curse of the Black Pearl*; for the latter, *Dead Man's Chest*. For the third movie, I'll use *At World's End*.

1. WAS THERE SUCH A THING AS CURSED AZTEC GOLD?

At the heart of the movie *The Curse of the Black Pearl* is a cursed chest of Aztec gold that once belonged to Spanish explorer Cortés. An amusing tale, but let's look at the true story the Aztecs and their gold.

Spain became a mighty sea power after plundering Aztec gold, thanks to conquistador Hernán Cortés who in 1519 took a relatively small force of 550 men to the capitol of the Aztec Empire, now known as Mexico City. Though the Aztecs didn't curse their gold, they understandably cursed Cortés and his men who, with the help of native allies, had mounted a fierce assault to conquer the Aztec people and plunder their vast stores of gold. Ironically, gold was of little value to the Aztecs, who called it "the excrement of the gods." The Aztecs used it only for ceremonial purposes. Cortés' lust for gold, though, soon became apparent to the Aztecs. Two years later, the Aztecs were conquered by the Spanish for their gold and resources.

Movie memorabilia from *Pirates of the Caribbean: The Curse of the Black Pearl,* a replica of Aztec gold, sold by the Noble Collection. On display at the Mariners' Museum.

A few decades later, the Spanish—a mighty economic power—had conquered all of Mexico, partly because of their wholesale plundering of the Aztec empire. At some point in the middle of all this looting, pirates (those scurvy dogs!) sailed the Caribbean, always on the lookout for slow-moving, treasure-laden Spanish galleons headed back home. As you can imagine, quite a bit of Spain's swag was promptly plundered by pirates. Where there be booty, there be pirates!

Note: My source for information about the Aztecs is an excellent article "Cortés and Aztec Gold" by Stuart Matthews (ICE Case Studies, Number 174, March 2006).

An Aztec artifact
on display at the
Mariners' Museum.

A bust of a pirate on display at the Mariners' Museum.

2. WAS THERE REALLY A PIRATE CAPTAIN NAMED BARBOSSA?

In *Curse of the Black Pearl,* we meet Hector Barbossa, the former first mate under Captain Jack Sparrow. After inciting a mutiny, Barbossa takes command and gives himself a promotion to captain. He then heads off to the Isla de Muerta to recover a chest of Aztec gold.

Little is known about Hector's background, but we know from seeing him in *Curse of the Black Pearl* that he's a wily man, fiercely intelligent, and known for honoring agreements. However, his greed leads to his downfall.

But you can't keep a good man down—nor, apparently, a bad one—so Barbossa makes a sudden and wholly unexpected appearance in *Dead Man's Chest* that puts him on center stage for the third film, *At World's End.* No doubt movie-goers will learn a lot more about the Machiavellian Hector Barbossa as he heads off to the South China Sea.

Of his character, Australian actor Geoffrey Rush told DVDTalk.com: "I got the feeling [Barbossa] was going to walk this very subversive line all the way through the movie. Absolutely relaxed, as if he was really touched by the sun, and maybe constantly a bit sort of tickled."

Described by a reporter for *Mercury News* as "the saltiest dog" in the *Pirates of the Caribbean* movie, Barbossa is an archetypal pirate: bad to the bone, clever, and greedy for all the ill-gotten gains he can find.

Although there was no pirate captain named Barbossa, there were two brothers named Aruj and Khayrad'din Barbarossa who terrorized the Mediterranean islands. The older brother, Aruj, was a redhead whose bright red hair and beard earned him the nickname "Redbeard." Barbarossa actually means "redbeard" in Italian. These two might have been the inspiration for Disney's Hector Barbossa.

3. Was There Ever a Real Pirate Ship Named the *Black Pearl?*

I t is the *Black Pearl*, not pirate plunder, that captivates Captain Jack Sparrow; the ship is permanently moored in his dark heart. However, according to a back story from the official *Pirates of the Caribbean: Dead Man's Chest* website (go to the drop-down menu and select "games" to mine the rich history behind its main character Jack Sparrow), the ship was originally named the *Wicked Wench*. Jack Sparrow was its captain, then under the employment of Lord Cutler Beckett of the East India Trading Company. Captain Sparrow was ordered to go to Africa and pick up cargo for transport to the

A resin statue of the *Black Pearl*. An open edition sold for $150 at the Animation Gallery at Walt Disney World Resort in Orlando, Florida.

Caribbean. Unbeknownst to Sparrow, it wasn't dry goods that filled his ship below deck; the cargo was African slaves. Jack refused his orders and set the slaves free. Consequently, he was hunted down by Lord Cutler Beckett, who promptly sunk Jack's ship, branded Jack's forearm with a "P" (for pirate), and put him in jail.

Now that you know the story about the fictional *Black Pearl*, do you think there was there ever a real ship called the *Black Pearl*? The correct answer is no, although it'd make a good name for a ship.

According to www.blackpearl.com, a black pearl is highly prized:

> The pearl is found in the South Seas; the black pearl is actually not black but, instead, ranges in color from silver to near black. Noted for its mirror-like surface, the round black pearl is the most prized of all—fewer than 2 percent of all black pearls can be found in this shape; most are tear-drop shaped, semi-round, or ringed. Ranging in size between eight to twelve millimeters, the highest grade given to a black pearl is "A" and prices can range from $530 for a pair of earrings to $3,670 for a necklace.

As Sparrow would attest, a ship named *Black Pearl* is surely a jewel among ships.

A log line used to measure the speed of the ship.
On display at the Mariners' Museum.

4. Were There Cannibals in the Caribbean?

In *Dead Man's Chest,* Captain Jack Sparrow is consumed by the notion of being a God to the Pelegostos tribe, an indigenous people located on an island in a remote corner of the Caribbean. What Jack doesn't realize, until it's too late, is that the Pelegostos tribe has developed a taste for an unusual meat delicacy sometimes called "long pig." The image of the young boy holding silver utensils in his hands, staring longingly and hungrily at Jack Sparrow, says it all: The Pelegostos people hunger for his flesh. When William Turner makes land on the island, it's no wonder that he hears a nervous parrot from Jack's crew squawk, "Don't eat me!"

Bon appétit.

Tourists wishing to explore Cannibal Island in the Caribbean will find their appetites unsatisfied. For those of you who hunger for the truth, here it is: There's no such island, there's no indigenous people called the Pelegostos tribe, and there's no historical evidence to suggest that cannibalism was practiced in the Caribbean. It is true, however, that Queen Isabella issued a prohibition against the Caribbean locals, whom she characterized as human flesh-eaters. She gave her subjects the authority "to arrest or capture any Indians . . . to do them any harm or evil to their persons or possessions" with the exception of "a people called Cannibales . . . [who] waged war on the Indians . . . capturing them to eat them as is their custom."

As a result, the Caribs were unjustly branded as meat-eaters of the worst kind, when in truth they were not. As Lyric Wallwork Winik pointed out (www.parade.com, July 26, 2006):

> Native Americans and other indigenous peoples want the Disney studio to walk the plank. A scene in *Dead Man's Chest* . . . depicts the Caribs—the islanders for whom the region is named—as cannibals. Charles Williams, chief of the remaining three thousand Caribs on the isle of

Dominica, says this is a false stereotype. In letters, early Europeans did refer to ritual cannibalism among the Caribs, but some historians now say it was exaggerated to justify their brutal treatment of the natives . . . . But critics fear that the film will condemn the Caribs to be remembered as cannibals.

Pirate skull. A window display at the
Disney Marketplace in Anaheim, California.

5. WHY WAS THE *BLACK PEARL* BEACHED ON ITS SIDE?

In *Dead Man's Chest*, the *Black Pearl* is beached on its side at Cannibal Island, the home of the Pelegostos tribe.

Although Jack Sparrow tells us that the *Black Pearl* is "well nigh uncatchable," the fact remains that like any ship that sailed in the warm Caribbean waters, she required ongoing maintenance to run at maximum speed. Speed was critical not only to catch up to a vessel they intended to attack, but also to make a fast escape if warships guarding a convoy pursued them. Obviously, pirates always felt the need for speed.

The preferred method of insuring adequate and timely maintenance was to put the ship in dry dock to allow easy access to the portions of the ship that were in constant contact with the water. Pirates, however, didn't have that luxury. Instead they had to find a place to beach the ship out of sight of the patrolling British navy. They would then careen the ship and complete repairs under the watchful eye of the ship's carpenter. An occupational hazard for the pirates, careening exposed the crew to attack from the British navy; therefore, it had to be done in an efficient and timely manner. As Dr. Kent Mountford points out in "Fouling Up" (www.bayjournal.com), the process was anything but easy:

> From the fifteenth century on, large trading vessels and naval ships became too large to be easily hauled. Bottoms were painted with tar or pitch, a byproduct of the charcoaling process.
>
> Ship planks were also smeared with hot tallow, stiff and waxy when chilled by seawater, which also reduced friction. Vessels still had to periodically be taken into a dry dock, though, to be scraped of their prodigious load of accumulated barnacles and other growth, where they were also checked for the worm.

Ships away from such facilities were taken into a quiet backwater and "careened." In this process, the ship's contents, much ballast, and most of her rig were backbreakingly removed to float her as high as possible. Tackles to anchors or other solid supports ashore were then used to haul her down—roll her on her side—to expose half of her bottom for cleaning.

This might include slightly charring the cleaned planks to dry and kill embedded worms, a process frequently aided by the hot tropical sun. She was then tarred and/or tallowed and refit for sea.

Often this involved replacing a plank or two that were affected by worms. For some reason, worms tend not to cross the boundary between adjacent timbers. For this reason, the keels of ships, which are most likely to have their protective coatings scraped off in grounding, were covered by a separate, sacrificial timber called the worm shoe.

Ships with clean bottoms sail faster, deliver more timely cargoes, and outmaneuver adversaries in combat.

Teredo navalis, commonly referred to as the shipworm, is not a worm, but an extremely destructive member of the mollusk family. Found in warm seas, this particular variation of shipworm ranges from eight to eighteen inches in length. This wood eater bores into wood, weakening and destroying it in the same manner as a termite. Because of the warm Caribbean waters, the careening process had to be done every few months; otherwise, both the ship's speed and its structural integrity would soon be severely compromised.

A tar bucket on exhibit at the Mariners' Museum.

6. WAS THERE A CODE OF BRETHREN AMONG PIRATES?

I n *Curse of the Black Pearl,* Elizabeth Swann attempts to save her pretty neck by demanding to see the captain of the pirate ship because the Code of Brethren specifically cites the right to parley, to be taken unharmed to the ship's captain to plead her case.

In truth, Caribbean pirates did subscribe to a set of specific guidelines that constituted law. Sometimes called articles of agreement, code of conduct, or simply the pirate's code, these articles laid out what was permissible behavior and what was not, including punishment for offenders. The pirate's code was often supplemented with additional articles specific to each ship that every pirate (press-ganged or otherwise) had to sign when joining the crew.

There are several notable differences between Disney's version of the code and the real thing. First of all, in the Disney version, the articles are said to be "more like guidelines," but in reality, they were inflexible and unforgiving. In the movie Elizabeth is told that she can't invoke parley because she is not a pirate. In real life, she would also have had a difficult time demanding it since there was no general clause that gave the right to parley. Elizabeth Swann, then, could not have reasonably expected to be taken to the ship's Captain to plead her case; nonetheless, the code would have protected her virtue. Pirate John Phillips, Captain of the *Revenge,* stated in his articles, "If at any time you meet with a prudent (that is, virtuous) Woman, that Man that offers to meddle with her, without her Consent, shall suffer present Death."

For His Ship *Revenge*, the Articles of Captain John Phillips

1 Every man shall obey civil command; the captain shall have on full share and a half in all prizes. The Master, Carpenter, Boatswain, and Gunner shall have one share and quarter.

2 If any man shall offer to run away, or keep any secret from the Company, he shall be marroon'd with one bottle of powder, one bottle of Water, one small Arm, and shot.

3 If any Man shall steal any Thing in the Company, or game, to the value of a piece of Eight, he shall be Marroon'd or shot.

4 If at any Time we should meet at another Marrooner (that is, Pyrate) that man shall sign his Articles without Consent of our Company, shall suffer such Punishment as the Captain and Company shall think fit.

5 That man that shall strike another, whilst these Articles are in force, shall receive Moses's Law (that is forty Stripes lacking one) on the bare Back.

6 That Man that shall snap his Arms, or smoak Tobacco in the Hold, without cap to his Pipe, or carry a candle lighted without lanthorn, shall suffer the same Punishment as in the former Article.

7 That Man that shall not keep his Arms clean, fit for an Engagement, or neglect his Business, shall be cut off from his Share, and suffer such other Punishment as the Captain and Company shall think fit.

8 If any man shall lose a joint in time of Engagement, shall have 400 Pieces of Eight: if a limb, 800.

9 If at any time you meet with a prudent Woman, that Man that offers to meddle with her, without her Consent, shall suffer Death.

7. DID PIRATES USE COMPASSES, MAGICAL OR OTHERWISE?

In both *Curse of the Black Pearl* and its sequel, *Dead Man's Chest*, a small but critically important tool is used for navigational purposes: a compass. However, Captain Jack Sparrow's compass is not what it seems. It appears to be an ordinary compass with a sundial to tell the time and a red arrow that points to true north. But anyone foolish enough to use it for that purpose will not find his way to a geographical port of call.

A compass on exhibit at the Mariners' Museum.

This one-of-a-kind compass that Jack got from Tia Dalma, a voodoo priestess, points not to true north, but to one's heart's center, one's true desires. For this reason, once people know of its true design, Jack's compass is highly coveted. Most people assume—and Jack is happy to have them think so—that the compass is simply broken. In fact, most of his fellow pirates accept the compass at face value. However, the few people that know better—notably Lord Cutler Beckett, who runs the East India Trading Company—will do anything to get their hands on it. If he had the compass, Beckett would be able to lord over the high seas. His plan is to find the Dead Man's Chest, which contains Davy Jones' beating heart, in order to gain control over him. Beckett would then command not only Jones and his nightmarish crew but the dreaded kraken as well.

A diminutive man with big ambitions, Beckett has his sights set on the grandest goals of them all: to rid the world of pirates and to command the passage of every seagoing vessel worldwide. All the world's ship captains must do what he says or face the terrible force of Davy Jones, his terrible crew (no quarter given), and (shiver me timbers!) the implacable kraken.

A working compass was an indispensable piece of navigational equipment in the sixteenth century because it always pointed north, yielding an accurate direction. In a pinch, a pirate could always construct an improvised compass if a lodestone and a needle were on board. The pirate would first rub the needle against the lodestone to magnetize it and then place it on a floating piece of cork in a small bowl.

A compass on exhibit at the Mariners' Museum.

Next to a compass, a detailed map was highly prized. Maps constructed by the Spanish were of greatest value because of their accuracy. In fact, one of the first things a pirate crew looked for when boarding a seagoing vessel was its map collection. Rather than see the maps fall into the hands of the enemy, Spanish ship captains preferred to throw them overboard—a great loss. But it would be an even greater loss if the maps were seized, copied for wider dissemination, and used against them. This happened in 1681 when Bartholomew Sharp seized a book of maps from a Spanish vessel. The invaluable maps were subsequently sent to England, where they were meticulously copied by hand and redistributed to English seafaring captains.

A map book on exhibit at the Mariners' Museum.

8. COULD THE BRITISH TROOPS FIRE FLINTLOCK RIFLES AND THEN FIRE AGAIN SECONDS LATER?

In *Curse of the Black Pearl*, Jack Sparrow makes good his escape from the British troops by temporarily holding Elizabeth Swann hostage. He then hoists himself into the rigging and swings around, so he can slide down a rope to a nearby street, where he sprints across a bridge and ducks into what he thinks is safe haven—the smithy where Will Turner works. Out of the frying pan and into the fire!

Luckily for Sparrow, the British troops are notoriously poor shots, unable to wing Jack with even one round. However, they make up for it with an amazing ability to reload and re-fire in a scant eight seconds!

Two flintlock rifles mounted on the wall of a replica ship moored at Jamestown Settlement.

Flintlock rifles and pistols were a big improvement over muskets, but they still took time to reload. In fact, a practiced soldier could reload in fifteen seconds, giving Jack barely enough time to escape. Since it takes Jack fifteen seconds from the time the first rounds are fired to the time he makes it across the bridge, the troops conceivably could have reloaded and re-fired if all had been trained to the same skill level—an

A reenactor prepares to fire a flintlock rifle at James Fort, Jamestown Settlement.

unlikely prospect. According to the Wikipedia (wikipedia.com), here's how to fire a flintlock rifle:

The operator loads the gun, usually from the muzzle end, with black powder followed by shot or a round lead ball, usually wrapped in a paper or cloth patch, all rammed down with a special rod, usually located on the underside of the barrel;

A cock or striker tightly holding a shaped bit of flint is rotated to half cock;

The flashpan is primed with a small amount of very finely ground powder, and the flashpan lid (or "frizzen") is closed;

The gun is now in "primed and ready" state, and this is how it would be carried hunting or going into battle. A safety notch at half cock prevents the hammer from falling by pulling the trigger. To fire:

The cock or striker is moved from half cock to full cock;

The gun is aimed and the trigger pulled, releasing the cock or striker holding the flint;

The flint strikes the frizzen, a piece of steel on the priming pan lid, opening it and exposing the priming powder;

The contact between flint and frizzen produces a spark that is directed into the flashpan;

The powder ignites, and the flame passes through a small hole in the barrel (a vent, or touchhole) that leads to the combustion chamber, igniting the main powder charge there; and the gun discharges.

In other words, given the length of time an experienced rifleman would require to reload, it helps explain how Jack escapes after the initial volley.

9. WHO WAS DAVY JONES?

In *Dead Man's Chest*, we meet Davy Jones, once human and mortal, but now inhuman and immortal. He commands the *Flying Dutchman*, a formidable ghost ship manned not by the usual motley pirate crew, but by a monstrous collection of once human, beastly looking creatures, including one whose head resembles that of a hammerhead shark. Commanding the wretched souls under him, Davy Jones sails the seven seas with impunity because he has the ultimate weapon, a sea beast that he summons from the depths. The kraken, which is the length of ten ships and seemingly part octopus, part squid, is capable of destroying any ship in mere minutes.

According to Tobias Smollett, author of *The Adventures of Peregrine Pickle* published in 1751, chapter XIII:

> By the Lord! Jack, you may say what you wool; but I'll be damned if it was not Davy Jones himself. I know him by his saucer eyes, his three rows of teeth, his horns and tail, and the blue smoke that came out of his nostrils. What does the blackguard hell's baby want with me? I'm sure I never committed murder, except in the way of my profession, nor wronged any man whatsoever since I first went to sea.
>
> This same Davy Jones, according to the mythology of sailors, is the fiend that presides over all the evil spirits of the deep. He is often seen in various shapes, perching among the rigging on the eve of hurricanes, shipwrecks, and other disasters, to which a seafaring life is exposed, warning the devoted wretch of death and woe. No wonder then that Trunnion[1] was disturbed by a supposed visit of this demon, which, in his opinion, foreboded some dreadful calamity.

[1]Commodore Hawser Trunnion is a character in *The Adventures of Peregrine Pickle*.

10. WAS THERE SUCH A THING AS A "DEAD MAN'S CHEST"?

In *Dead Man's Chest*, Davy Jones, the captain of the *Flying Dutchman*, buried a small chest containing his beating heart. The chest itself had ornate locks that could not be forced open; in fact, it could only be opened with a special key, which Jones kept on a string around his neck.

While there are some references in pirate books to a "dead man's chest," they should not be confused with the title of the second Disney film. A dead man's chest was slang for a wooden coffin. The historical reference, however, is Dead Chest Island in Tortuga, the site where the infamous pirate Blackbeard marooned some of his crew, whom he considered mutinous. The historical reference later became a literary reference when Robert Louis Stevenson used it in *Treasure Island* as part of a pirate chant: "Fifteen men on the dead man's chest, Yo ho ho and a bottle of rum!"

Actual sea chests used to store valuables were larger than the chest shown in the Disney film. A typical chest would be twenty-nine inches wide, nineteen inches deep, and twenty-two inches high; it would be constructed of all wood, usually pine or ash, with brass fixtures and leather straps. Inside, there would be a wooden holding tray. The chest would, over time, develop a rich patina, giving the wood a luxurious, golden color. The chest could be secured by a standard lock.

An oil painting by well-known pirate artist, Howard Pyle, titled *Marooned*, originally published in *Howard Pyle's Book of Pirates*.

11. DID CAPTAIN BARBOSSA HAVE TO INCITE A MUTINY TO TAKE CONTROL OF THE *BLACK PEARL?*

When *Curse of the Black Pearl* opens, we see Captain Jack Sparrow standing on a yard (a horizontal spar on a mast), etched against the sky. With one hand on the lip of the crow's nest and the other on his hip, he sights a British ship moored off Port Royal. The camera swings around and we get our first good look at Jack, who looks resolute and fearless, as the camera moves in for a close-up of his face.

We are in for a visual joke: Jack is not, as you would assume, in command of the mighty *Black Pearl*. Instead, he commands a leaky fishing dory named *The Jolly Mon* that belongs to a female pirate named Anamaria. As Jack puts it, he "borrowed" the boat without her permission and had full intentions of returning it one day. Yeah, right.

A close-up of an oil painting by well-known illustrator N. C. Wyeth, depicting *Captain Bill Bones* for the Scribner edition of *Treasure Island*.

So, the question arises: Why *isn't* Jack in command of his ship, the *Black Pearl*? As it turns out, Jack's former first mate on board, Hector Barbossa, incited a mutiny, took command of the *Black Pearl,* and marooned him on a remote island in the Caribbean.

And another question arises: Did Barbossa have to incite a mutiny, or was there an alternative?

In *Dead Man's Chest,* after Jack makes his escape from a Turkish prison by breaking through his floating coffin (a real dead man's chest), he uses a skeleton's leg as a paddle and heads to the *Black Pearl* where he expects to be greeted with huzzahs for his triumphant return. The ship's crew, however, is in a dark mood. Instead of engaging in honest pirating, the ship, under Jack's command, has been hotly pursued by the British navy, suffered a hurricane, and been diverted to the Isla de Muerta. The crew wants to know "Where's the loot, the treasure?" Jack rhetorically responds, "Is that how you're all feeling, then? Perhaps dear old Jack is not serving your best interests as captain?"

The parrot candidly answers for the crew. "Awk! Walk the plank!" However, silver-tongued Jack talks his way out of trouble, for now.

Pirates didn't follow the law of the land—neither British nor New World. The law they followed was a set of rules known under several names, but most commonly called the pirate's code. There was not a single code but several codes, written as articles by different pirates, such as Edward "Blackbeard" Low, John Philips, and Bartholomew "Black Bart" Roberts—the latter being the model for the code adopted in *Pirates of the Caribbean* movies.

The first article in Roberts' Code was that "Every man has a vote in affairs of moment; has equal title to the fresh provisions, or strong liquors, at any time seized, and may use them at pleasure, unless a scarcity, no uncommon thing among them, makes it necessary for the good of all to vote a retrenchment."

In other words, pirates ran a true democracy, and if the crew wasn't happy with the current ship's captain, there was no need to mutiny; he was simply voted off the ship. Therefore, First Mate Hector Barbossa could simply have put the matter to a vote and ended it right there.

12. DID PIRATES CONSULT VOODOO PRIESTESSES?

In *Dead Man's Chest*, we meet Tia Dalma, a voodoo priestess who lives at the mouth of the Patano River on a Caribbean island. She's exotic, preternaturally young, and possesses great powers. She's also an old flame of Jack Sparrow, though when she meets Will Turner for the first time, she understandably warms up to him. Given Dalma's isolated neighborhood, it's not likely that she meets normal-looking men on a regular basis, so we can forgive her heightened interest in Will.

It is Tia who will, along with Jack's friends—Elizabeth Swann, Will Turner, and some former crewmembers of the *Black Pearl*—make sail to the ends of the Earth to bring Jack back from Davy Jones' locker, chronicled in *Pirates of the Caribbean: At World's End*.

Those who journey to Haiti will search in vain for the swamp-like neighborhood seen in *Dead Man's Chest*. The climate of Haiti is tropical and bears no resemblance to the Louisiana Bayou that inspired the geographical setting for Tia Dalma's shack, a haphazardly constructed wooden structure. Furthermore, though Haiti does have numerous rivers, you'll not find one named Patano.

Those who search in the historical records for any connection between pirates and voodoo as practiced by Haitians are also doomed to disappointment. There is nothing that shows any connection between the two.

The swampy neighborhood of Tia Dalma—and, perhaps, the inspiration for Tia Dalma herself—can be found in the Louisiana bayous. As Kristin Mouk (author of "Bayou Tours: A Guide to the Louisiana Outdoors") points out,

> The word bayou originated from the term bayuk, the Louisiana French word for "small stream." By definition, a bayou is a watercourse, usually the offshoot of a river

A powder flask with ornate decorations, on display at the Mariners' Museum.

or lake in a lowland area. It is a sluggish or stagnant creek, frequently flowing through swamp terrain. The term is used mainly when referring to areas in the delta region, the area near the mouth of the Mississippi River. In comparison, a swamp is a low-lying, marshy wetland, and is usually forested and seasonally flooded.

According to Dennis William Hauck in *Haunted Places: The National Directory* (1996), Maria Laveau was the Voodoo Queen of New Orleans:

> She led voodoo dances in Congo Square and sold charms and potions from her home in the 1830s. Sixty years later she was still holding ceremonies and looked as young as she did when she started. Her rites at St. John's Bayou on the banks of Lake Pontchartrain resembled a scene from Hell. . . . She had a strange power over police and judges and succeeded in saving several criminals from hanging.

It would be hard to find a more colorful and bewitching voodoo priestess in New Orleans than Leveau, who was the most powerful figure of her kind in the city's history. She was even said to have clairvoyant powers: She palmed herself off as a seer and reputedly had other mysterious powers as well.

Could Leveau have been the real-world inspiration for Tia Dalma? In Disney's fantastic world, anything is possible.

13. DID PIRATES ROUTINELY DESTROY ENEMY SHIPS?

In *Curse of the Black Pearl,* the film opens with a British frigate plying Caribbean waters, making its way through dense fog, as an unconscious young boy floats on a piece of ship's wood. As it turns out, he's the sole survivor of a pirate attack. The merchant vessel he was on is now half submerged, a flaming wreck.

"Everyone's thinking it. I'm just saying it . . . Pirates," Joshamee Gibbs. Gibbs says darkly, as he looks at what remains. Lieutenant Norrington, though, dismisses the claim. He thinks it was merely a shipboard accident, since merchant vessels were "heavily armed" and the powder stored below deck could have simply ignited, destroying the ship.

Boats are lowered to search the site for signs of other survivors, but there are none. The only clue as to what happened is a black ship sailing away that only young Elizabeth sees. Its flag is the Jolly Roger with its distinctive human skull and cross cutlasses—the telltale sign of a pirate ship.

Shiver me timbers, I'm thinking it and saying it: Them was pirates!

Pirates customarily didn't destroy the ships they attacked unless they faced stiff resistance and had no other alternative. They obviously preferred to commandeer a bigger and better ship into service, adding it to the fleet.

A shot pouch containing gun powder, used with flintlock pistols and rifles. On display at a building in James Fort, Jamestown Settlement.

A close-up of a miniature re-creation of a fifty-gun British ship handmade by August F. Crabtree, on display at the Mariners' Museum.

14. Did pirates steal ships?

When there's a will, there's a way to hijack a ship. In *Curse of the Black Pearl*, Captain Jack Sparrow and Will Turner make it appear that they are stealing the Commodore's flagship the *Dauntless*, which is clearly too big a ship for two men to hijack; in truth, the goal was not the *Dauntless*, but the fast brigantine *Interceptor*, which could be minimally manned by a crew of two. After disabling the main rudder to the *Dauntless*, Will and Jack make good their escape.

Pirates didn't buy ships: They simply stole them, by force, and not by subterfuge, which is how Jack and Will assume control of the *Interceptor*. After gaining control of the ship, Jack and Will sail to Tortuga, on the north coast of Hispaniola, the second largest island in the Caribbean.

A miniature model of a Spanish galleon,
on display at the Mariners' Museum.

A close-up of a miniature Spanish galleon,
on display at the Mariners' Museum.

A close-up of the open gunports on a miniature
Spanish galleon, on display at the Mariners' Museum.

15. Did pirates use shipboard guns to attack shore-based British forts?

In *Curse of the Black Pearl*, under the cover of darkness and bad weather, the *Black Pearl* heads toward the harbor of Port Royal and assumes a firing position in mid-harbor. As Commodore Norrington and Governor Swann walk on the ramparts, Swann hears an unfamiliar sound. "What's that?" Swann asks, clearly puzzled.

Norrington looks toward the harbor and tackles Swann as he yells, "Cannon fire!" A ball then strikes nearby as Norrington covers the governor with his body.

"Return fire!" shouts Norrington, and the shore-based fortification opens up with its large guns.

At Jamestown Settlement in Jamestown, Virginia, where three sixteenth-century replica ships are moored, I asked a historical interpreter whether or not pirate ships sailed into harbor and attacked a town, port, or military fortification. She replied that pirates usually went under cover of darkness, with a false flag, and gunports closed. Then, after an ideal firing position was selected, the pirate ship would show her true colors by opening up the gunports and begin a barrage, a ship-to-shore attack to soften up the enemy, prior to launching a ground assault.

Round shot on display at the Mariners' Museum.

Guns on wooden carriages at James Fort, Jamestown Settlement.

That scenario is exactly what is depicted in the *Curse of the Black Pearl,* which took its cue from the Disney theme park boat ride on which it was based.

As a former field artilleryman, it strikes me that the pirate ship would, so to speak, be a sitting duck in the water. Within range of long guns from shore fortifications that could return a greater volume of fire and with larger balls, the pirate ship (it would seem) would be damaged to the point where she couldn't maneuver back out to open sea, if she managed to avoid being blasted out of the water.

For the most part, the ship's guns were used in ship-to-ship combat, in broadsides, which could irreparably damage or destroy an enemy ship at close range. Fighting on the sea played to a pirate's strengths. Though I'm sure pirate ship-to-shore attacks were conducted, I'm willing to bet that the majority of the attacks were sea-based.

16. Did the British brand pirates?

In *Curse of the Black Pearl,* Commodore Norrington offers to shake Jack Sparrow's hand, but in fact uses it as a ruse to inspect Jack's left forearm to see whether he's been branded with the letter "P" to indicate he's a pirate. Norrington discovers that Jack is branded, which prompts the Commodore to remark that Jack must have had a run-in with the East India Trading Company.

The British didn't brand pirates because there'd be no reason to do so. Neither did any other military power during that time. When pirates were captured, they were simply put on trial and, if convicted, they were sentenced to be hung until dead.

Branding pirates is an interesting notion though, one that Lord Cutler Beckett favors. According to *Pirates of the Caribbean: The Visual Guide,* Beckett is the kind of fellow who likes to leave his mark on a pirate forearm—with a branding iron in the shaped of the letter "P."

As to whether or not it's true, who knows? I've found no authoritative record of pirates being branded, but the film's scriptwriters, Ted Elliott and Terry Rossi, are pretty adamant about it; presumably, they did a lot of research.

17. Why Would a Seaman Be Justifiably Alarmed if a Cat Was Let Out of Its Bag?

In *Dead Man's Chest*, "Bootstrap" Bill Turner volunteers to flog his son rather than have the ship's sadistic bosun enjoy causing horrific wounds with each blow of the cat-o'-nine-tails.

Flogging was a routine punishment not only on pirate ships, but on merchant marine ships and in the British navy as well. The hand-held device used was a short stick with nine knotted ropes called the cat-o'-nine-tails. Particularly effective at inflicting pain, it could be used to flay a man alive, if the number of strokes was high. Keep in mind flogging was reserved for *minor* punishments! In the British navy, the floggee made his own whip, which consisted of nine ropes with knots. Usually, a dozen lashes was considered adequate punishment. Those who served, voluntarily or not, on pirate ships or merchant marine ships got whatever the captain thought was warranted; sometimes it was dozens of lashings—enough to kill a man.

When the cat was not in use, it was stored in a canvas or leather bag, which led to the nautical expression, "Let the cat out of the bag." When the cat was out of the bag, it was surely used to flog someone.

Because the severity of the wounds varied depended on the vigor employed by the flogger, it was preferable, if possible, to get someone you knew to handle the distasteful chore. As was the case with Bootstrap, he knew that he could pull his punches, so to speak, in flogging his own son. But if the bosun wielded the whip, the first blow would rip the flesh off his son's back and subsequent lashes would turn the back into raw bleeding flesh. Will would then be at risk of dying from infection—a commonplace occurrence.

The practice of the using the "cat" gave rise to another nautical expression, "I'll scratch your back if you'll scratch mine." So a man who was about to be flogged always preferred to have a friend do it; he, in turn, would reciprocate when the opportunity arose.

18. WAS THERE EVER A SHIP CALLED THE *FLYING DUTCHMAN?*

In *Dead Man's Chest,* Davy Jones commands the *Flying Dutchman,* a ghost ship that rises out of the ocean's depths to appear before doomed mariners who must make a difficult choice: to accept the natural order of life and choose to die—or join its ghostly crew in servitude for a century. In other words, the doomed sailor would have to choose, as the saying goes, between the devil (Davy Jones) or the deep, blue sea.

The ship is commanded by Davy Jones and his crew is recognizably human in form but clearly mutated, their bodies and faces resembling sea creatures, their flesh encrusted with barnacles and shells. Jones himself is described by actor Bill Nighy who plays him as half-crab and half-octopus.

There are several versions of the Davy Jones legend, but in the most popular one, a Dutch ship captain named Vanderdecken is piloting his ship during a bad storm off the coast of South Africa, near the Cape of Good Hope. Stubborn to the last, he pledges to round the Cape no matter what, but the storm takes a toll: All hands are lost. The ship must now—depending on the legend you believe—sail forever around the Cape of Good Hope or sail the seven seas.

Furthermore, legend states that to see the ship is a bad omen because it means disaster will soon strike. Though there have been several sightings over the years of UFOs (Unidentified Floating Objects), notably phantom ships that mysteriously appear and disappear without a trace, there's been no recorded instance of imminent disaster experienced by the ship's sailors.

19. WHAT WAS A LETTER OF MARQUE?

In *Dead Man's Chest*, Lord Cutler Beckett, who heads the East India Trading Company, wants to strike a deal with Jack Sparrow. In exchange for Jack's bewitched compass, Beckett offers him a letter of marque.

What will it be, Jack? Deal . . . or no deal?

Bearing the royal seal of the King of England, the letter of marque was in effect a license to steal. An enemy ship—from a country at war with England—was fair game. With a letter of marque, Jack Sparrow could loot, pillage, and burn to his heart's content, though he would have to account for his plunder and give ten percent to the East India Trading Company. Jack would be legit: a privateer, not a pirate. But then Jack wouldn't have the same cachet, would he?

The letter of marque allowed a nation to augment its own naval forces at no additional cost. The English and also the Dutch, the French, and the Belgians issued their own letters of marque.

In Jack's instance, he could sail the high seas and attack Spanish ships. The Spanish, of course, felt quite differently. If caught by the Spanish, Jack would find himself and his crew in dire straits. Remember the Spanish Inquisition? The Spanish were particularly skilled in torture techniques.

Fans of nautical tales who want to know more about letters of marque should read Patrick O'Brian's novel *The Letter of Marque*. Its plot, according to the publisher:

> Captain Jack Aubrey, a brilliant and experienced officer, has been struck off the list of post-captains for a crime he did not commit. His old friend Stephen Maturin, usually cast as a ship's surgeon to mask his discreet activities on behalf of British Intelligence, has bought for Aubrey his former ship the *Surprise* to command as a privateer, more politely termed a letter of marque. Together they sail on a desperate mission against the French, which, if successful, may redeem Aubrey. . . .

20. WHAT WEAPONS DID PIRATES CARRY?

In both *Curse of the Black Pearl* and *Dead Man's Chest,* the pirates are armed with a number of weapons during ship battles and ground assaults.

Once on board an enemy vessel, pirates liked to employ a campaign of shock and awe, intended to subdue the enemy as quickly as possible. Though armed to the teeth, pirates knew boarding an enemy ship entailed considerable risk, especially if any resistance was mounted. In fact, because of the risk that the first pirate to board took, he had his first pick of weapons afterward—if he survived the attempted boarding.

Keep in mind that hand-to-hand combat is difficult enough on land and particularly dangerous at sea, since ships were always in motion and usually rocked side to side. In no particular order, here's what pirates carried and why:

1. A flintlock rifle. This accurate weapon was usually fired by an accomplished marksman. The target was usually officers or key personnel. By picking off the leaders first, it meant that the crew was more likely to surrender. A simple and effective strategy: Cut off the head (the leader) and the body (the crew) will soon follow.

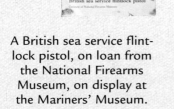

A British sea service flintlock pistol, on loan from the National Firearms Museum, on display at the Mariners' Museum.

2. A flintlock pistol. Very effective at close range, it also served as a club, which is why its butt was usually made of heavy brass. The pirate Blackbeard carried several pistols on his person, tied with silk ribbons, so he could repeatedly fire without reloading, which was time-consuming and impractical under the circumstances.

3. A boarding axe. A particularly fearsome weapon, it was also used to cut ropes, cut rigging to disable the ship, and open up banded cargo.

4. A cutlass. The preferred bladed weapon, this short sword was standard issue. If a pirate had nothing else as a weapon, he'd almost always have a cutlass, which didn't require the skills needed to handle a longer sword.

5. A dagger. Short and deadly, the thin dagger was ideal for close-in fighting and below deck where it could be pulled out from beneath one's clothing and used to stab. Below deck, where it was dark, the dagger was especially deadly because you'd never see it coming.

A display of pirate weapons on display at the Mariners' Museum.

6. A blunderbuss pistol or rifle. Distinctive in design because of its belled muzzle that flared out at the end, this intimidating weapon was ideally suited for small quarters. While inaccurate, it was capable of distributing many musket balls in a wide spread, like a shotgun

A bandolier with powder measures and shot pouch on display at the Mariners' Museum.

shell. The larger blunderbuss rifle was an effective anti-personnel weapon, spraying defenders.

7. Stink pots. Stuffed with rags, these produced a large volume of smoke, which helped mask the boarding effort.

8. Grenades. Usually made of ceramic with a primitive fuse, these could weigh up to three pounds. They were used more to shock than to create casualties, but were problematic because their fuses didn't always work.

21. WERE PIRATES HUNG?

In *Curse of the Black Pearl,* while headed into Port Royal, Jack Sparrow passes a gruesome sight: the skeletal remains of three pirates hanging from a beam positioned between a pair of rocks over the water. Just in case the visual imagery wasn't enough to send the right message, the sign makes it clear: "Pirates, ye be warned."

A pirate had no desire to "dance the hempen jig" (being hung with a hemp rope as one's legs jerked spasmodically), but he knew hanging was his eventual fate if caught.

The "publick gaol" (public jail) in Colonial Williamsburg, where Blackbeard's pirates were incarcerated for two weeks while awaiting trial.

In the opening scene of *Curse of the Black Pearl,* pre-teen Elizabeth Swann says, "I think it would be rather exciting to meet a pirate."

A grim-faced Lieutenant Norrington responds, "Think again, Miss Swann. Vile and dissolute creatures, the lot of them. I intend to see to it that any man who sails under a pirate flag, or wears a pirate brand, gets what he deserves: a short drop and a sudden stop."

Just to make sure Swann gets the message, the ever helpful Joshamee Gibbs, who later becomes a pirate on the *Black Pearl,* mimes to her the sight of a man being hung: his hand jerking on a rope as his eyes and tongue comically bulge out of his face.

Death by hanging was in fact the traditional punishment meted out to a pirate. Afterward, the corpse would be preserved with tar and put on public display, usually in a gibbet to insure the skeletal remains would remain in place—a stark reminder to those who contemplated joining the ranks of pirates.

The view from inside the jail cell that Blackbeard's pirates briefly enjoyed in Colonial Williamsburg.

The actual cells where Blackbeard's pirates were held in Colonial Williamsburg. (Note: Each cell has two windows, including one on the door and one looking out on an open field; each room is fairly small, with a food slot and a three-tiered wooden toilet in the corner. Shackles hang from the walls.)

The toilet in the corner of the jail cell where Blackbeard's pirates were held in Colonial Williamsburg. (Note: The wooden cutout on top covers the toilet when not in use. The cell was lined with straw.)

22. DID PIRATES USE MAROONING AS A PUNISHMENT?

Jack Sparrow is one of the unluckiest pirates ever to sail the high seas. Case in point: Sparrow, the former Captain of the *Black Pearl*, saw his first mate, Hector Barbossa, stage a mutiny and take over the ship. For his troubles, Jack is made "the governor of an island," meaning he was put ashore on an island and left to die. Jack makes his escape, but as chronicled in *Curse of the Black Pearl*, he is once again marooned, though this time he has lovely company: a pragmatic, feisty Elizabeth Swann.

Thanks to Elizabeth's foresight, they don't have to face the dismal prospect of starvation on the remote island. She uses the rum to set a fire that catches the attention of the British navy patrolling nearby waters on a search and rescue mission for her. Sparrow, however, is still distressed. Where is all the rum?

The eventual fate of most marooned pirates, being reduced to skeletal form. On display at the Mariners' Museum.

Remember this important safety tip: Rum is flammable, according to a warning label on Bacardi Rum: a fact that Danielle Alleyne, who is suing the company, learned the hard way. According to AP/Fox News (July 26, 2006),

> A woman who was allegedly severely burned by flaming rum during a Bacardi promotion sued the wine and spirits producer, claiming the product was defective and dangerous. . . . A bartender, who was not identified in the lawsuit, was pouring shots when a customer lit a menu on fire and placed it in the stream of alcohol.

Bartholomew "Black Bart" Roberts is credited as the author of the pirate's code, sometimes called the pirate's code of conduct, which lays out in eleven rules what's expected among pirates, and what to expect if you violate one of the rules.

Item two states,

> Every man shall be called fairly in turn by the list on board of prizes, because over and above their proper share, they are allowed a shift of clothes. But if they defraud the company to the value of even one dollar in plate, jewels, or money, they shall be marooned. If any man rob another, he shall have his nose and ears slit, and be put ashore where he shall be sure to encounter hardships.

In addition to theft or robbery, a pirate could also be marooned for cowardice in battle. It's ironic that a pirate, whose trade is theft and robbery, could be pilloried for stealing among pirates, but there was at least honor among thieves.

That "he shall be sure to encounter hardships" is a foregone conclusion. In real terms it meant that a pirate was given a flask of water sufficient for one day, a pistol, enough powder, one ball, and nothing else. He would find no help in his surroundings either; a pirate was typically put ashore on a deserted island with little or no vegetation, a island with rocky outcroppings, or just a spit of sand. There would be no fresh water, no food, and no shelter from the elements. In other words, it was a slow, agonizing death, which is why he was grateful for the option of using his pistol as a quick and painless way to permanently resolve the situation.

As for the chances of another pirate ship spotting the marooned pirate, they were slim to nonexistent; besides, even if he were spotted, the presumption was that the person marooned was put there for a reason, so why bother rescuing him?

Those hapless souls who were marooned immediately put their efforts toward finding water, food, and shelter. Nonetheless, marooning was a death sentence. Either the lack of sustenance would kill the victim or, when things got unbearable, he would end his prolonged misery by killing himself.

A Howard Pyle painting, titled *Marooned,* is an iconographic illustration of this state of despair: Painted in shades of dark yellow, ochre, and brown, a pirate is seated on the sand, his arms clasped around his drawn-up knees and his head down.

23. DID PIRATES ATTACK MERCHANT SHIPS?

In the opening scene of *Curse of the Black Pearl,* the flaming remains and wreckage of a ship are grim reminders that plying the high seas is risky business. Though it's not possible to tell what kind of ship it was from the wreckage, chances are it was a merchant ship, since young Will Turner was on board, probably as a cabin boy.

A popular pirate saying: No prey, no pay. This meant that a pirate only got paid when there were ships to raid. A popular misconception is that pirates only looted ships for gold. Truthfully, while pirates were always interested in silver and gold coins and artifacts, they didn't expect to find a sea chest filled with money. According to David Cordingly, author of *Under the Black Flag,* pirates most often "liberated" household goods and other supplies: "sails, pump-bolts, log-lines, needles, twine, kettle, [a] frying pan," and "fourteen boxes of candles, and two boxes of soap, together with a flying-jib, flying jib-boo, flying-jib-halliards, main halliards, anchor and cable, and several carpenter's tools."

Obviously, pirates had to keep their own ship seaworthy, and also replenish their supply of victuals (food supplies). They could not just pull into the nearest port because it might be hostile territory.

Since merchant ships had no combat-hardened troops and only a few guns for defense, they weren't capable of defending themselves against pirates that typically outnumbered them: Depending on the size of the ship, the crew of a pirate ship averaged eighty men.

A typical merchant ship had a crew of approximately twenty men, with six guns for protection. Fake guns and gunports were sometimes painted on to suggest the ship had more armament than it really did. As it takes a minimum of four men to man a gun, the crew obviously couldn't fight and sail. In short, it was no contest. Most merchant ships simply surrendered. Imagine the terror of seeing your lightly

Household goods in a sea chest, the most common booty stolen by pirates. On display at the Mariners' Museum.

Pearls, silver and gold coins, jewelry, and other valuables—the fabled treasure chest sought by pirates. On display at the Mariners' Museum.

manned merchant ship boarded by dozens of armed-to-the-teeth, battle-hardened, death-or-glory pirates.

Though pirates were well-versed in ship-to-ship and hand-to-hand combat, they preferred not to fight unless they had no other choice. Intimidation was a major factor used to frighten the merchant ship crew into submission. Why risk combat if you could achieve the desired end result without fighting? As Lao Tzu wrote in *The Art of War*, supreme excellence in battle is being able to subdue the enemy without fighting him.

Sometimes raising the Jolly Roger (the black or red flag) was sufficient. It signaled that pirates were going to board, whether you liked it or not. The only question was, did you want to chance fighting to the death—or acquiesce and hope they'd take the cargo and leave? It was well known that if you chose to resist and fight that you'd be in for a bloody, no quarter given, fight to the death, with pirates holding the upper hand.

If a pirate attacked the right Spanish ship, one headed back across the Atlantic to Europe, they could strike it rich. Pirate Bartholomew "Black Bart" Roberts struck gold when his ship attacked one such ship in a convoy. According to David Cordingly, his haul was "90,000 gold moidores [a Portuguese gold coin], a cross set with diamonds which was intended for the King of Portugal, chains and jewels of considerable value, and a cargo of sugar, skins, and tobacco."

In truth, pirates lived hard, died young; most pirates were in their twenties or early thirties and probably left an ugly looking corpse. But those occasional rich hauls—especially gold ingot bars weighing up to five ounces, or Spanish doubloons—made the risk worth taking. (In January 2007, gold was valued at $623 an ounce, according to www.monex.com.)

24. DID PIRATES KEEP PARROTS ON BOARD?

In *Curse of the Black Pearl,* Captain Jack Sparrow and William Turner attempt to recruit a crew. One prospective employee among them, Mr. Cotton, is a mute man whose tongue had been cut out. His parrot, they are told, speaks for him.

If there's one animal associated with pirates, it's a parrot. Colorful, talkative (capable of imitating human voices), and companionable, parrots were in fact part of the permanent landscape of pirates.

Whether or not most pirate parrots were as talkative as Long John Silver's squawky parrot named Cap'n Flint, who knows? We do know, however, that pirates kept parrots as pets and also found them to be in great demand in Europe.

25. WERE ALL PIRATE FLAGS BLACK WITH A SKULL AND CROSSBONES DESIGN?

In *Curse of the Black Pearl*, Elizabeth Swann (and apparently no one else) sees a black ship pulling away into the sea mist after destroying another hapless merchant ship. The black ship's flag is the iconic skull and cross sabers against a black background—a pirate's flag.

Though not all pirate flags were black, all of them sported symbology specifically designed to strike fear into the heart of any sailor who realized that a pirate attack was imminent.

Skulls, crossbones, cross sabers, a figure holding an hourglass, a red skeleton, and a pirate figure were all iconographic and specific to flags that identified the pirate.

For instance, a traditional skull and crossbones might signal the arrival of Stede Bonnet, Edward England, Henry Every, Walter Kennedy, Christopher Moody, Richard Worley, or Emanuel Wynne.

The flag flown by the *Black Pearl* in *Pirates of the Caribbean* is the same one used by "Calico" Jack Rackham, who in 1720, along with his crew, was captured by authorities and taken to be hung in Port Royal.

Prisoner irons on display at the entrance of the public jail in Colonial Williamsburg.

26. What Forms of Punishment Did Pirates Inflict?

In *Dead Man's Chest*, Will Turner is flogged. He is surely thankful it is at the gentler hands of his father and not a sadistic member of the *Flying Dutchman* crew. In *Curse of the Black Pearl*, both Jack Sparrow and Elizabeth Swann are marooned on a remote Caribbean island, where Jack was briefly marooned before.

Both flogging and marooning were common punishments, but they were not the only way to enforce discipline. Pirates proved that there's no end to human ingenuity when it comes to making someone suffer.

1. Secured in irons. Pirate ships lacked brigs, so instead pirates simply fastened wrist and leg irons on the victim and put him below deck. Believe it or not, this was preferable to being put above deck, since the punishing Caribbean sun and wind-whipped rain were often forms of torture in themselves.

2. Sweating. This particularly nasty punishment involved a victim running around a ship's mast, often to the point of exhaustion, while onlooking pirates jabbed him with cutlasses and other sharp instruments.

Leg irons on display at the entrance of the public jail in Colonial Williamsburg.

3. Keelhauling. This was by far the most barbaric and justifiably the most feared practice. The victim's hands and feet were bound and he'd be dragged under the keel of the ship (from port to starboard), usually encrusted with razor-sharp barnacles, and then pulled out of the water. If he didn't drown or get attacked by a shark, he'd later die of infection.

27. WHAT STRATEGIES DID PIRATES USE TO ATTACK SHIPS?

I n one of the most dramatic, eye-catching sequences in *Curse of the Black Pearl*, the British are attacked by the *Black Pearl*. The cursed crew use an unorthodox method of getting to the British ship. They walk on the surface of the ocean bottom and then climb up the sides of the British vessel.

Pirates always observed the three S's when attacking: speed, stealth, and surprise. Speed was not only essential for catching up to the prey but also for escaping, since another enemy ship, possibly a well-armed warship, might be in the area. Stealth and surprise are always tactical advantages. By running up false colors, the pirate ship could get close enough to assess the tactical situation. In order to get as close as possible, a pirate ship might also cover its gunports or carry cargo on deck suggestive of a civilian vessel. What armament does the other ship have? How many crewmembers are aboard? What kind of vessel is it? What kind of cargo might it be carrying? Then, when the pirate ship determined its prey was worth attacking, the Jolly Roger was raised, the gunports uncovered, and the pirates called out to the enemy ship: surrender . . . or die, for resistance is futile!

It was always best to capture a ship and its crew intact because it could take hours to properly examine and offload the ship's hold, not to mention interrogating the crew if there was any possibility of money or valuables aboard beyond ship supplies, medical supplies, or household goods.

If the ship's crew decided to resist, the pirates opened up with broadsides intended to cripple, not sink, the enemy ship. Grappling hooks would then be used to pull

Bar shot and round shot
on display at the Mariners' Museum.

them together, though this was not done from port-to-starboard (along-side), since the respective riggings could get damaged. Marksmen from the pirate ship would then use the flintlock rifle to pick off the ship's captain or officers. Bar or chain shot would be used to disable the ship by tearing down its rigging to prevent escape. If the bar or chain shot

A swivel gun mounted on a replica ship at the Jamestown Settlement.

weren't enough, round shot would be fired in a broadside, which usually damaged the ship's structural integrity. As the hooks drew the ships together, the pirates would prepare to board. Well armed with stink pots, grenades, rifles, and cutlasses, their path might be cleared by a few blasts from the guns using anti-personnel shot from blunderbuss rifles that sprayed the deck. In the smoke and confusion, the pirates boarded and hand-to-hand combat ensued.

After the battle was won and the ship thoroughly sacked, the only decision was what to do with the crew. This varied from captain to captain. The general rule was that if no resistance was offered, the pirates had no compelling reason to injure or kill the crew, and they were usually left unharmed. In cases of mounted resistance, the vic-tims could expect little or no mercy.

Moreover, press-ganging sailors and, especially, skilled tradesmen was common. A pirate crew suffered from attrition and needed to

replenish its ranks. The remaining crew would be forced to sign the ship's articles, making them pirates who, if caught, could be hung by the authorities. (The tradesmen were generally the exception. They usually did not sign the ship's arti-cles and, when caught, pleaded that they were involuntarily pressed into service, thus escaping punishment.)

Closed gunports on a replica ship at the Jamestown Settlement.

28. DID PIRATES BURY THEIR TREASURE?

In *Curse of the Black Pearl*, treasure is hidden by Captain Hector Barbossa and his crew. They've accumulated more wealth than they could ever spend, even with their extended lifetimes. The location of the treasure is kept secret to protect their ill-gotten gains: coins, jewelry, gold artifacts, plates, pearls, and of course the cursed Aztec gold that prevents them—at least until the curse is lifted—from enjoying their ill-gotten gains.

It's certainly true enough that pirates sometimes struck it rich, notably Thomas Tew and his crew, in 1693, when a raid yielded sufficient booty that each member of the crew became instant millionaires: $3.5 million dollars (in today's currency), to be exact.

Caribbean pirates, though, lived a short and brutal life. When they weren't plundering on the high seas, they were on land, in places like Tortuga. Spending money as drunken sailors, they guzzled booze, gambled, and lived for the moment because they didn't know, or care, what tomorrow will bring.

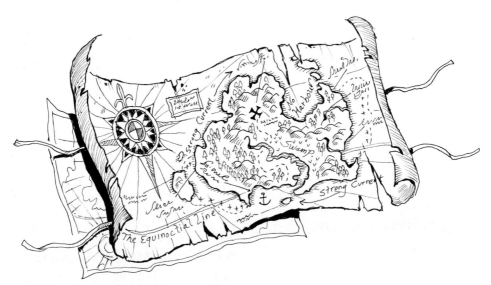

Pirates typically divided up the booty after a raid, so there was little incentive to save for a rainy day. For this reason, the notion that there are sea chests full of gold found in the rotting hulls of sunken pirate ships is fanciful; moreover, there was no incentive to bury it on land, though that doesn't stop people from believing in, and prospecting for, pirate booty.

As nautical expert David Cordingly pointed out in a Disney documentary (on disc two, *Curse of the Black Pearl*), "The thing about buried treasure is that I don't believe in it." He affirms that there are accounts of buried treasure—notably pirate Thomas Kidd, who buried his loot on Gardner's Island off the New York coast—but in the main, there's very little else to substantiate this popular myth.

Some people in Florida feel differently, however; according to www.treasurelore.com, there's gold in them thar hills, though there's a lot more gold down in Davy Jones' locker. The difference is that a good metal detector, a lot of time, and luck are needed to discover the former; the latter is far more difficult (and dangerous) to retrieve because it's sunken treasure, a different kettle of fish. Laden with chests of gold and silver, sunken Spanish galleons are most frequently found off the Florida coast, since that was the principal route the Spanish ships would take: across the Gulf of Mexico, down the west coast of Florida, around its tip (after a brief stop in Cuba), halfway up the eastern coast of Florida, and then to Spain.

The sunken treasure is yours for the taking, right? Wrong! A private individual doesn't have the resources to mount a recovery expedition, which can take years and millions of dollars using the latest high-tech gadgets to locate and excavate valuable artifacts. Not to mention the state of Florida exercising its claim on any booty discovered within its territorial waters, and insurance companies demanding repayment of payoffs made centuries ago.

A chest laden with treasure, on display at the Mariners' Museum.

29. DID PIRATES GAMBLE WITH DICE ABOARD SHIPS?

In *Dead Man's Chest,* Will Turner uses a ruse to find out the location of the key needed to open the Dead Man's Chest, which contains the beating heart of Davy Jones himself. Like son, like father, the elder Will Turner joins in the game after his son makes the bet. Both lose, but young Will finds out what he needs to know. Davy Jones keeps the key on a string around his neck.

The three main vices that constantly drained pirates' free time and money were booze, women, and gambling, especially during shore leave. The dice game has its historical basis in a poem written in 1798, the *Rime of the Ancient Mariner,* by Samuel Taylor Coleridge. In the poem the ancient mariner sees a ghost ship with only two occupants: a Specter-Woman (Life-in-Death) and her Death-mate (Death). Life-in-Death wins the game of dice, with the mariner himself as the prize.

30. Did Pirates Press-Gang Their Victims?

In *Dead Man's Chest*, Jack Sparrow regretfully tells Elizabeth Sparrow that her beloved Will Turner has been forced to join the crew of the *Flying Dutchman*, that he was press-ganged. Did pirates actually force others to join their crew against their will?

Pirates did indeed press-gang, but it depended on whether the person in question would be a useful member of the crew. Tradesmen (called "artists") were those with a vocational trade that could be put to good use on board a ship. A carpenter was highly valued because he was essential to keeping any boat afloat. His principal duties were to keep the ship's seams from leaking and to repair wood damaged in battle. A doctor was also a highly valued member of the crew. A cooper, a barrel maker, was also a mission-essential tradesman. The food and water stored in barrels required constant maintenance because the ship's shifting movements affected their integrity. As for others, it depended on whether they were sailors or civilians. The sailors on a merchant marine ship were always good replacements, but sailors on a privateer ship were even better than merchant mariners, because they were sea savvy with the added advantage of having combat experience. Civilians, however, were of little use on a pirate's ship, so the pirate captain had to make a decision. If they were lucky, they'd be put ashore. If not, they'd be killed and simply dumped overboard.

Most of those press-ganged had to sign the articles of the ship, stating that they would abide by the rules set by its captain. Better that, they reasoned, than face immediate death.

31. WAS PORT ROYAL AN ENGLISH HARBOR DURING THE GOLDEN AGE OF PIRACY?

A setting in *Curse of the Black Pearl* and *Dead Man's Chest*, Port Royal figures prominently in both movies. It is the home base of Commodore Norrington in the first film (he suffers a fall from grace in the second film); it is the home of Governor Swann and his daughter Elizabeth; it is where blacksmith Will Turner makes his living; and it is where Jack Sparrow makes his triumphant return, sailing into port in a small fishing boat. Port Royal is a thriving, bustling seaport under strict English control.

Port Royal was exactly as shown in the *Pirates of the Caribbean* films, but its early history was anything but savory. Today tourists who go to Jamaica will see a historical marker put up by the Jamaica National Heritage Trust. The marker tells a chilling but fascinating tale:

> Once called "the richest and wickedest city in the world," Port Royal was also the virtual capital of Jamaica. To it came men of all races, treasures of silks, doubloons, and gold from Spanish ships, and looting on the high seas by the notorious "Brethren of the Coast" as the pirates were called. From here sailed the fleets of Henry Morgan, later lieutenant-governor of Jamaica, for the sacking of Camaguey, Maracaibo, and Panama; he later died here, despite the ministrations of his Jamaican folk-doctor. Admirals Lord Nelson and Benbow, and the chilling Edward "Blackbeard" Teach, were among its inhabitants. The town flourished for thirty-two years until twenty minutes to noon, June 7, 1692. It was partially buried in the sea by an earthquake.

Port Royal, to put it mildly, had a very unsavory reputation prior to the establishment of English rule. In fact, it had a lot in common with Mos Eisley, a spaceport seen in *Star Wars* (the original film), populated by space pirates. As Obi-Wan Kenobi observed, "You will never find a more wretched hive of scum and villainy. We must be cautious." The same could certainly be said about Port Royal, which was home to pirates, wanton women, and cutthroats of every kind. After plundering a merchant ship, pirates would return to Port Royal and throw their money away. As recounted in Charles Leslie's *New History of Jamaica*:

> Wine and women drained their wealth to such a degree that, in a little time, some of them became reduced to beggary. They have been known to spend 2,000 to 3,000 pieces of eight in one night . . . They used to buy a pipe of wine, place it in the street, and oblige everyone that passed to drink.

Today, Port Royal and its collection of aged fortifications play host not to pirates but tourists interested in them. Places like Buccaneer Restaurant and Buccaneer's Roost, with a Jolly Roger flag flying overhead, pay tribute in name only to its inglorious but colorful past. The real pirate sites, such as Gallow's Point, where many pirates met their ends after dancing the hempen jig, is now covered over with mangroves. It's peaceful and quiet, and there's little to suggest that it was, at one time, a wretched hive of scum and villainy. Those interested may wish to keep informed about the Port Royal Heritage Tourism Project (www.portroyal-jamaica.com), which intends to restore the city to its former glory, on the order of Colonial Williamsburg, a living museum and major historical and cultural destination for tourists. The proposed restoration of Port Royal won't be a sanitized interpretation but, instead, a recreation of what it was during its heyday, a bustling, important seaport under British rule.

32. HOW DID PIRATES EMPLOY SHIPBOARD GUNS?

In both *Curse of the Black Pearl* and *Dead Man's Chest,* broadsides are fired from guns on board the *Black Pearl* and the *Flying Dutchman.* In one dramatic show of force, the *Black Pearl* fires on the town of Port Royal and one of its six forts, Fort Charles.

The most common usage was to fire broadsides against an enemy ship, if its crew failed to surrender. A pirate ship would also sail into port with its gunports closed, assume a firing position, and fire directly on fortifications or the town itself.

The ammunition used included:

Grapeshot for a ship's gun, on display at the Mariners' Museum.

1. Round shot. An iron ball weighing anywhere from four to twelve pounds, depending on the size of the pirate ship. This was used to blast holes in an enemy ship. Typically, the pirate ship would pull up alongside the enemy ship and, if necessary, fire away with round shot.

2. Bar shot. At first glance, you'd be hard pressed to figure out what it's used for because it's so oddly shaped. An iron bar with balls at the end or a variation thereof, it was used to cut rigging on a ship, "the sails, masts, booms, yards, stays, and lines of a sailing vessel, or its cordage only," according to *Encyclopedia Britannica.* In other words, it was used to cripple the ability of the ship to maneuver, to sail.

3. Canister shot. This was not against the enemy ship itself but against its crew. It was comprised of small musket balls (called shot), used to mow down anyone unfortunate enough to be standing in its wide spray path. Its effect was

similar to a claymore mine with tiny pellets, or an artillery round with steel fleshettes (called a "beehive" round).

The idea was to use the ammunition in concert, to disable but not destroy the enemy ship, and also injure or kill its crew. This would greatly reduce the likelihood of your own casualties in hand-to-hand combat.

On the use of broadsides: In both *Curse of the Black Pearl* and *Dead Man's Chest,* we see the classic ship-to-ship battle in which guns are firing through gunports, usually in volleys, to disable the enemy ship.

Pirates usually preferred not to fire the guns on board unless there was no other choice: If the enemy didn't surrender without a fight, it became necessary to subdue him. Pirates used guns as a last resort because there was always the possibility that the iron balls would sink the ship, making recovering booty impossible. Under ideal circumstances, the ship would be taken intact to allow adequate time for searching; depending on the size of the ship, this could be a lengthy process. Pirates needed time to interrogate the crew to determine if there was money on board and where it was hidden.

The guns were referred to by the size of the iron ball they fired. They could fire a one-pounder, two-pounder, four-pounder, six-pounder, eight-pounder, twenty-four-pounder, and thirty-two-pounder. The guns themselves ranged in weight from six hundred to five thousand pounds.

The shipboard guns used in the seventeenth century had many significant disadvantages:

1. A gun was heavy and had to be mounted on a wooden carriage with four wheels. When the guns were fired they recoiled several feet. (Ropes were used to secure it from recoil.)

2. It took an experienced gun crew to load, fire, and reload. It also took time and a lot of practice to train a good gun crew.

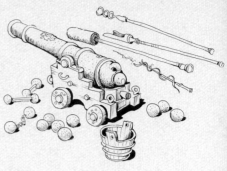

3. Even with an abbreviated gun crew it would take a minimum of four men (ideally six men) to prepare a gun, fire it, and reload it. This meant that these men could not be employed in the boarding party, where the manpower was critically needed.

4. The guns could only be fired when the ship was level. Otherwise, the wheeled guns would roll around on the deck.

5. The several minutes it took for an experienced gun crew to reload opened up a window of vulnerability for the enemy ship to fire back.

6. The standard tactical strategy was to initially fire with a broadside: all guns firing at once to achieve maximum shock value and damage to the ship itself.

7. The gun's range varied depending on the amount of powder charge used, but the maximum range to maintain accuracy was only a few hundred yards. Therefore, the best use of round shot was from ship-to-ship—close range.

8. The guns were ineffective as a long range weapon. (By the way, in case you're wondering, the rotating guns firing like a Gatling gun as seen in *Dead Man's Chest* are Hollywood fiction.)

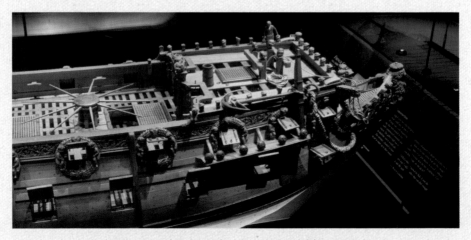

Detail on a miniature ship hand-carved by August F. Crabtree, on exhibit at the Mariners' Museum.

33. DID PIRATES MAKE THEIR VICTIMS WALK THE PLANK?

If you were to take an informal street poll and ask passersby, "What punishment did pirates most often employ?" most people would respond "walking the plank." It's easy to understand how someone would get this idea, since it's a staple of popular pirate-themed books, most notably *Peter Pan* and *Treasure Island*. Even pirate book author/illustrator Howard Pyle added to the legend, stating in his article for *Harper's Weekly* ("Buccaneers and Marooners of the Spanish Main" in 1887) that the infamous pirate Blackbeard often made his victims walk the plank. He also pro-

vided an illustration so iconographic that it's been reprinted in numerous books about pirate history.

Years later, film director George Lucas paid homage to this popular but erroneous pirate myth in his space fantasy *Star Wars*, in which Luke Skywalker and Han Solo are forced to walk the plank—not into water but into the gaping, tooth-

The deck of the *Godspeed*, a replica ship moored at the Jamestown Settlement, Jamestown, Virginia.

some mouth of a creature embedded in desert sand. Not surprisingly, the plank-walking legend resurfaces in *Curse of the Black Pearl*, when Elizabeth Swann and Jack Sparrow are forced by Captain Barbossa to take a short walk off the *Black Pearl*.

Walking the plank seems like just the kind of punishment a sadistic pirate would mete out. But there's no evidence to back it up. In fact, pirates who used hit-and-run tactics didn't have the luxury of time to stand around and watch a very reluctant victim walk the plank. Pirates lacked subtlety; they usually killed the victim and unceremoniously dumped him overboard.

Below the thunders of the upper deep,
Far, far beneath in the abysmal sea,
His ancient, dreamless, uninvaded sleep
The Kraken sleepeth: faintest sunlights flee
About his shadowy sides; above him swell
Huge sponges of millennial growth and height;
And far away into the sickly light,
From many a wondrous and secret cell
Unnumbered and enormous polypi
Winnow with giant fins the slumbering green.
There hath he lain for ages, and will lie
Battening upon huge sea-worms in his sleep,
Until the latter fire shall heat the deep;
Then once by man and angels to be seen,
In roaring he shall rise and on the surface die.

—"The Kraken" by Alfred Lord Tennyson, written in 1830

34. WAS THERE A SEA BEAST LIKE THE KRAKEN?

In *Dead Man's Chest,* the murderous crew aboard Davy Jones' ship the *Flying Dutchman* have at their command a weapon more powerful than all the guns she carries. They control the kraken, a gigantic sea monster whose tentacles are so powerful that it can crush a ship or snap it in two. Commanded by Davy Jones himself, the kraken arises from the depths to surface just long enough to probe the topside of the doomed ship with its tentacles, snatch unwary sailors, tear down masts, and crush the ship, sending its crew to a watery grave. Imagine having a power such as that at your command! According to the Disney version, Davy Jones himself is the only one who can summon the kraken.

The scenes in *Dead Man's Chest* of the kraken rising from the deep and attacking ships are riveting to watch. One can easily see how a sea creature of such size and strength could reduce a ship to tinder. The length of ten ships (up to two thousand feet long) according to Disney myth, the kraken is nature's deadliest submarine capable of remaining submerged until it surfaces to attack with deadly force. Its suckers can rip the flesh off a sailor's face, its tentacles can snap masts and crush ships, and its razor-sharp teeth and circular mouth make short work of any sailor unlucky enough to survive the initial attack.

But is there such a thing as a giant squid? Yes, but not quite as gargantuan as Disney would like us to believe. To be sure, if there were such a thing as a giant squid the length of five football fields, it could easily destroy any wooden ship in history. But according to *National Geographic,* the longest giant squid on record measured fifty-nine feet. Impressive, of course, but hardly in the same league as the sea beastie conjured up through the magic of computer-generated imagery by Disney Imagineers.

35. COULD A PIRATE WALK UNDERWATER BY HOLDING AN INVERTED BOAT OVER HIS HEAD?

In *Curse of the Black Pearl,* Jack Sparrow and Will Turner use subterfuge to make their way from the shores of Port Royal to the British ship, HMS *Dauntless.* By inverting a small boat, approximately eighteen feet in length, they resolutely march into the water. By virtue of the air pocket created by the inversion, they are able to breathe underwater until they board the ship.

Although the undead pirates that man the *Black Pearl* can walk underwater because they're skeletal and weighed down with cutlasses and other weapons, the natural buoyancy of the human body is such that both Jack and Will, without the boat, would simply float to the surface—unless they had weights to hold them down. It's likely that the idea for using the boat as an improvised underwater breathing apparatus came from the 1952 film *The Crimson Pirate.*

Interestingly, the technique itself has merit, once the buoyancy problem is solved. An online encyclopedia (http://encarta.msn.com) notes:

> The earliest reference to underwater diving techniques occurs in the manuscripts of the Greek philosopher Aristotle. The manuscripts refer to a diving bell used by the forces of Alexander the Great to clear the harbor at Tyre in 332 B.C. This contraption, shaped like a bell, was actually a large wooden barrel that a diver could place over the head and upper body while walking on the bottom of the sea. Underwater, the pressure of the air trapped inside the barrel kept out any water that might enter. This displacement created an airspace where the diver could breathe and see.

36. ARE JACK SPARROW'S SABER AND PISTOL HISTORICALLY ACCURATE?

In *Curse of the Black Pearl*, after Jack Sparrow saves Elizabeth Swann from drowning, he is captured by Commodore Norrington and his saber and pistol are confiscated. Norrington, who quickly determines this is the infamous Jack Sparrow, pulls the pirate's sword out of its scabbard and comments, "I half expected it to be made of wood. You are without doubt the worst pirate I've ever heard of."

A display of swords in scabbards at James Fort, Jamestown Settlement.

"At least you've heard of me," Jack retorts.

Norrington would soon eat his words and grudgingly admit to one of his men that he clearly underestimated Sparrow, that ol' Jack was in fact one of the best pirates he had ever seen.

Among swords, a saber was the weapon of choice for boarding an enemy ship because it was short and perfect for close-up fighting.

The pistol was also a staple, but pirates preferred to carry more than one because of the possibility of misfire. Capable of a single shot before reloading, the pistol required powder that, when damp, might not ignite. Blackbeard reportedly carried three or four pistols with him, tied to his belt with silk so that he could shoot and drop.

Pirates also carried a dagger that measured approximately eighteen inches in length. Carefully concealed, the dagger was a dangerous close-up weapon, especially below deck where space precluded the use of a longer blade.

A flintlock pistol on display at James Fort, Jamestown Settlement.

More than likely, Jack wore a brace of pistols, primed and ready to fire, a cutlass, and a concealed dagger, so he would be prepared for any contingency, above or below deck.

37. WERE THERE FEMALE PIRATES?

In *Curse of the Black Pearl*, Jack Sparrow and Will Turner are recruiting potential crew from a port in Tortuga, a haven for pirates. Among those recruited is a female pirate named Anamaria. She slaps Sparrow in the face because he had stolen her small fishing boat, the *Jolly Mon*. Since the *Jolly Mon* sunk when docked at Port Royal, she'll never see her boat again. However, when Jack promises that she'll get a bigger, faster boat, she reluctantly agrees to join his motley crew.

In addition to Anamaria, who made no bones about her true gender, Jack's crew also includes Elizabeth Sparrow, who is dressed in male sailor's clothing like a cabin boy. Jack, of course, sees through her ruse and now has two female members among his crew.

Female pirates Mary Read and Anne Bonny await trial (photo courtesy of Pirates in Paradise Festival in Key West, Florida).

Although there were women pirates, they were very clearly the exception, not the rule. In most cases, a young woman might pass for a young teenage boy and thus secure a berth on a pirate ship. But what was the inducement? Life on board a ship was no pleasure cruise; amenities were nonexistent; and the bathroom facilities were primitive. Below deck the atmosphere was even more inhospitable. Pirates bunked wherever they could among the ship's supplies and food stores. In other words, it was dark, cramped, smelly, and offered no creature comforts. There were, however, lots of creatures, both desired and undesired: livestock intended for slaughter, sailors' pets, mostly cats and dogs, though some had more exotic and colorful animals like parrots and monkeys, and lots of rats.

"Calico Jack" Rackam's crew included Anne Bonny and Mary Read, both of whom cut colorful swaths in pirate history. Their gender, however, didn't protect them from the power of the courts. Both women were tried and condemned to hang, but after sentencing they informed the court of their pregnancies. Since the courts couldn't hang a "woman with child," at least until after she had given birth, both female pirates received temporary reprieves. (For the record: Mary Read died in prison before the sentence could be carried out, and there's no record of what happened to Anne Bonny.)

38. WAS IT BAD LUCK TO HAVE A WOMAN ON BOARD?

In *Curse of the Black Pearl,* the movie opens with a pre-teen Elizabeth Swann looking out over the water from a British fighting ship. A ship's hand, Mr. Joshamee Gibbs, remarks darkly, "It's bad luck to have a woman on board, too. Even a miniature one," referring to Miss Swann.

The "logic" behind that thinking was that women were considered the weaker sex. They not only needed to be harbored from life's vicissitudes but were considered needless distractions on board a ship.

A female ship figurehead on display at the Mariners' Museum.

39. DID PIRATES WEAR PEG LEGS?

Davy Jones wears a peg leg, a prosthetic device made of wood. Is this realistic?

Unfortunately, this is very realistic. Life at sea during the golden age of pirates was anything but romantic, especially when it came to shipboard accidents. Hurricanes, storms at sea, slippery decks, and falling heavy equipment all contributed to on-deck and below-deck disasters. Unfortunately, in the event of a serious injury, the only solution was immediate amputation. This would be performed by the ship's surgeon if one was on board or, in a pinch, the cook.

The only bright side was that if the injury was sustained during combat in the line of duty, the code specified that the pirate would be rewarded monetarily for his loss. For example, if the pirate was one of Blackbeard's crew on *Queen Anne's Revenge,* article eight of that ship's code would specify that "If any man shall lose a joint in time of Engagement, shall have 400 Pieces of Eight: if a limb, 800."

According to David Cordingly, author of *Under the Black Flag,* one piece of eight (also called "eight reales") was worth the equivalent of $23 today, so by today's standards the valuation of a limb would have been approximately $18,400.

40. DID PIRATES REALLY DRINK RUM?

In *Curse of the Black Pearl,* Jack is marooned with Elizabeth Swann on an island, but at least he has his rum—for a while, anyway. While Jack sleeps off the rum's effects, Elizabeth takes the opportunity to use it as fuel for the fire, to signal the Royal Navy patrolling the waters searching for her. Not surprisingly, Jack is a little upset. As every savvy pirate knows, rum is what keeps the boat afloat. "What happened to the rum?" Jack asks groggily, after awakening from a hangover.

In *Dead Man's Chest,* Jack Sparrow goes below deck on the *Black Pearl* to get another bottle of rum, where he meets Bootstrap Bill, a former shipmate bearing bad news for him and his crew.

A History of Rum
by Sonya Alvino

The history of rum is inseparably linked to the sea, and its legacy is traced through the naval explorations of the sixteenth century, the slave trade, and the seafaring tales of the pirates who made a name for themselves on the back of many a rum-infused journey.

So romantic is the history of rum that it has long since been adopted as the drink of the working-class man throughout the world. This might be due to its association with the "fighting man" and the strength of victorious sailors fighting for the New World; or, perhaps, the defeat of Napoleon's fleet by Admiral Nelson's rum-drinking crew at the crucial battle of Trafalgar; or maybe the swashbuckling freedom tales of Caribbean pirates handed down through the centuries. Whichever, it is clear that rum has had a checkered history, undeniably linked to the riskier business of the day.

One of the main challenges of sixteenth-century sea voyages was providing crews with a liquid supply to last long journeys. Navy captains turned to the most readily available sources of the day—water and beer—with no real discrimination made between the two. Water contained in casks was the quicker of the two to spoil (due to algae growth), but beer also soured when stored for too long. Royal Navy sailors took to drinking their rations of beer first and water second, sweetening the spoiling water with beer or wine to make it more palatable. The longer the voyage, the larger the cargo of liquid required, and the more serious the problems of storage and spoilage became.

As seafaring vessels entered the Caribbean, captains took advantage of a cheaper and more readily available source of liquid sold by local sugar-cane plantations called "kil devil"—a foul-tasting by-product of sugar-cane processing, which later became known as rum. Rum quickly replaced beer rations and became an official ration on British navy ships from 1655 onwards.

Reportedly, these rum rations were causing such "rum-bullion" (drunkenness and discipline problems) among the seamen that in 1740 vice-admiral Edward Vernon issued an order to dilute rum rations with sugar and lime juice. This could be why the new mixture was reputed to fight off "lurgy" or scurvy. Vernon's nickname of "old grog" was applied to the new cocktail and rum then became known as "grog."

Dilution ratios varied aboard different ships over time, but the tradition continued until "Black tot day" on July 30, 1970, when the last ever "Up Spirits" rum measure was served aboard British Royal Navy ships.

Many of the famous pirates of the seventeenth and eighteenth centuries were recruited from plundered naval ships and consisted of sailors tired of poor pay, limited rum rations, nutritional diseases, and the harshness of their captain. With the promise of an equal share in any loot pirated, it's not hard to see why many chose a pirate's life of freedom, democracy, and frivolity. Notorious pirates Captain Kidd and Morgan Nelson both started their seafaring careers as naval officers.

Pirate captains capitalized on the popularity of rum to gain the favor of their crews, and rum was often the larger cargo and preferred bounty. The search for rum was constant and, without the Crown's strict rum-rationing guidelines, many a vessel was plundered as a result of its crew being too drunk to take proper charge of the ship.

So favored was rum that the scarcity of it could be the cause of out and out rebellion on pirate ships. The meanest of all pirates from history, Blackbeard, once stated: "Such a day; rum all out. Our company somewhat sober; a damned confusion amongst us! Rogues a plotting. Talk of separation. So I looked sharp for a prize [and] took one with a great deal of liquor aboard. So kept the company hot, damned hot, then all things went well again."

It is therefore no accident that rum became so popular around the most prosperous pirating "Golden Era" of 1650 to 1740. This was also, coincidentally, about the time that the slave trade began to take off and New England entered the triangle between Africa and the Caribbean, with rum being used as the currency of the slave trade.

Molasses would leave the Caribbean for New England to be distilled into rum, which would be shipped to Africa in exchange for slaves, who would then be shipped to the Caribbean to tend the sugar plantations and harvest more sugar cane, to be converted to molasses. So prolific was this industry that by the mid-seventeenth century, tiny Rhode Island had more than thirty distilleries, twenty-two of them in Newport, and in Massachusetts sixty-three distilleries produced 2.7 million gallons of rum.

Sugar, rum, slaves, sailors, and pirates all had a hand in the development of the New World, from whichever standpoint you look at it. So intrinsic is the relationship between all of these components that it is hard to determine which would exist without the other.

41. DID PIRATES HAVE FEASTS FOR GUESTS?

In *Curse of the Black Pearl,* Elizabeth Swann is given an unappetizing choice; she may either dine with the crew sans clothes or dine clothed with Captain Barbossa. To the crew's dismay, she chooses a candlelit dinner with Barbossa, though not without a few reservations.

Even though Barbossa is a pirate to the bone, he puts out a good spread complete with bread, fresh fruit, chicken or turkey, desserts, seafood (fresh fish, shellfish, eel), and a small roast pig. Although famished, Elizabeth Swann eats daintily, with fork and knife, as any eighteenth century lady would. But when Barbossa tells her that she need not stand on ceremony, she starts eating with gusto, tearing off a chicken leg and ripping off the meat with her teeth. When Barbossa offers wine, she accepts. But when he offers an apple, she's suspicious, thinking it's poisoned—an understandable supposition, since Barbossa has not partaken. Elizabeth's wrong though . . . dead wrong.

Among the US military services, the Navy serves (in my estimation) the best chow. Because I've dined on naval vessels and in Army and Air Force mess halls, I can make the comparison. The reason, I believe, is that when you're on board a ship, the quality of the food is a major morale booster. Good food means happy sailors; bad food means unhappy sailors with just another thing to complain about. Consequently, food in the naval mess halls *must* be uniformly excellent. For the same reason, the cuisine on a cruise ship is similarly notable. With celebrated chefs, a wine steward, and world-class cooks, the food on a cruise ship is fit for a king.

Unfortunately, food onboard a pirate ship was a morale destroyer. Since pirates lacked means of food preservation except for salting, the longer they were at sea, the more likely the food and water would go bad. In the worst case scenario, if the food went bad and they were unable to catch any seafood, it meant softening up leather and eating

A brick kitchen on the replica ship *Godspeed* at the Jamestown
Settlement. (Note: Larger ships had room to construct a brick kitchen,
but smaller ships had to use barrels filled with sand for cooking.)

leather goods—their sole food. No question about it, there were good
reasons why pirates didn't necessarily look forward to dinner.
According to some historians, pirates preferred to eat below deck in
semi-dark conditions because it meant they couldn't see the weevils
that infested their meals. As for that magnificent spread Barbossa had
prepared for Elizabeth Swann, it's not bloody likely!

A movie prop from *Dead Man's Chest*, on exhibit at the Disney Gallery in New Orleans Square, Disneyland Park, Anaheim, California. "The Bone Throne is the official seat for the leader of the Pelegostos Tribe. The Throne is constructed from the remains of prior tribal leaders."

SECTION II

A PIRATE'S LIFE FOR YOU

Learn how to talk and swagger like a pirate! How to dress like a pirate! Find your sealegs! Discover sea cruises, pirate festivals, and museums worth your time! And get the "skinny" on Disney's Pirates of the Caribbean theme park ride and rollicking film!

A painting by N. C. Wyeth for *Treasure Island.*

1. How to Speak Like a Pirate

If you're like most landlubbers, chances are pretty good, me bucko (friend), that ye only know one pirate word: *arr!*, which ye usually speak with one eye shut, your teeth gnashed, and a forefinger hooked. Why bother to learn to speak like a pirate, anyway? It's not as if you're going to be needing that skill anytime soon—or might you? The people who need to know their stuff cold are the pirate reenactors. In fact, they take great pride in getting everything down just right, from every stitch of clothing to the working vocabulary of those in the maritime trade.

The rest of us might find speaking like a pirate useful if we were to dress up and attend a pirate festival, go on a pirate cruise where there's booty for the best-dressed and well-spoken pirate, or want to show our true colors (black or red, of course) on "Talk Like a Pirate Day," September 19.

Because pirates were usually experienced merchant seamen or privateers-turned-pirates, it helps if you have a nautical background or know your way around a ship. But chances are good you don't, so here's a quick crash course on what you need to know to separate yourself from the scurvy dogs who think it'd be a prelude to a romantic evening to "kiss the gunner's daughter."

Insulting Terms

Bilge rat. A reference to the furry creature who lived in the lowest part of a ship. A great way to start a fight, if you're in the mood.

Scurvy dog. A general, all-purpose insult.

Greetings and Warnings

"Avast ye!" is usually spoken forcefully. It means "Stop!" or "Be quiet!" You say it to get someone's attention.

"Aye, aye, sir!" means you've been given an order and you are complying.

"Huzzah!" Hooray or hurrah!

People

Boatswain or bosun. Usually called the bosun, he had several duties, the most important of which was taking charge of the ship's anchors, sails, rigging, cables, etc. When on deck he passed on the captain's orders. Below deck, he was in charge of the ship's supplies.

"Calico" Jack. The nickname for John Rackham, known for his trademarked white cotton shirts.

Carpenter. A highly skilled and prized tradesman, often press-ganged into service on a pirate ship for his ability to help maintain the ship and its structural integrity, and supervise repairs after an engagement at sea.

Cook. A low-ranking position on board a ship. This duty was not assigned on the basis of the pirate's culinary skills; instead a physically disabled pirate who couldn't fight was normally assigned this duty.

Barrels on display (with tobacco in the background) at James Fort, Jamestown Settlement.

Cooper. He made casks and maintained them at sea to insure their integrity, since they were the principal means to store water, rum, food, and gunpowder. (Think Tupperware without its sealing advantages.)

Landlubber (sometimes just a lubber). A person who doesn't have his sea legs, distinguished by one's ability to walk with the rolling gait of an experienced sailor. It also implies a civilian, someone whose nautical knowledge doesn't hold water.

Quartermaster. The Quartermaster is second-in-command and is in charge when not in combat. He's the crew's representative in all matters. He usually attained captaincy when another ship was attacked and then captured, requiring a new ship captain.

Sawbones. Nickname for the surgeon who set bones, performed amputation, etc. (*Not* to be confused with a doctor, a medical man.)

Places

Bilge. The lowest part of the ship, known for accumulating refuse both solid and liquid. The breeding grounds for rats, as well.

Crow's nest. A high point, usually on the main mast, from which a sailor could see for up to twenty miles.

The crow's nest of the *Godspeed*, a ship replica, at the Jamestown Settlement.

Things

Backstaff. This was used by the navigator to determine distance by measuring the height of a landmark.

Ballast. This is weight carried in the hold of the ship to enhance its stability. In the seventeenth century, this included stones and full barrels of water.

Bar shot. Fired from guns, these bars were specifically intended to disable a ship by destroying her rigging and shrouds. A very effective close-in weapon.

A backstaff used for navigational purposes to determine latitude, on display at the Mariners' Museum.

Black Spot. The Black Spot was first used in *Treasure Island* by Blind Pew, who gives it to Captain Billy Bones. The paper had a large Black Spot, which signified he would soon die; the reverse side told when.

Blunderbuss. The blunderbuss was an effective, short-range weapon. It was normally braced against one's hip. It is similar to today's sawed-off shotgun.

Brig. Short for a brigantine, a brig is a sailing ship with two masts. Its slang definition: the ship's prison. Most ships didn't have prisons, so prisoners were "clapped in irons."

Broadside. A broadside is a tactic used to disable an enemy ship. It is a simultaneous firing of all guns to achieve maximum shock, awe, and damage. Broadsides from large naval vessels—a ship with one hundred guns for example—could inflict considerable damage in one volley.

Cackle fruit. Slang for a chicken's egg.

Cards. Pirates often play cards to pass time on board a ship, since pirates had to fight boredom when not in combat.

Cat-o'-nine-tails. A whip used to torture sailors, it had nine strands of knotted rope. It could be used to flay a man alive. In fact, because of the blood it drew, it was necessary to "clean the cat's tails" to keep the strands free of coagulating blood.

Cutlass. A short, razor-sharp sword prized by pirates because of its effectiveness as a close-in weapon for hand-to-hand combat.

Dagger/dirk. A short, thin, and exceedingly sharp blade usually hidden in one's clothing or boot that could be used for stabbing or throwing.

Doubloon. A highly prized coin minted by the Spanish by melting Aztec gold. It weighed approximately one ounce.

Eyepatch. These were often worn by those who suffered from eye injury after viewing the sun directly while using a navigational tool called a cross-staff.

Fathom. A unit of measure equaling six feet that is used to determine depth.

Flagship. The commander's ship, usually the biggest. Pirates who had a small fleet designated one of them as the main ship.

A hand lead on display at the Mariners' Museum. "Weighing ten pounds with a twenty-five fathom line marked at intervals, the hand lead is used for soundings and to determine bottom composition."

Flogging. Onboard punishment used to enforce discipline involving using a short whip with multiple strands of rope called a cat-o'-nine-tails.

Galleon. A large three- or four-mast ship invented by the Spanish to cross the transatlantic route from the New World back to the Old World. Relatively slow and ungainly, it served as either a warship with dozens of guns or, because of its large hold, a cargo ship.

Graveyard of the Atlantic. The final resting place for hundreds of ships and thousands of sailors that went to Davy Jones' locker. The Graveyard of the Atlantic is located off North

Carolina's Cape Hatteras, where warm water from the south mixes with the cold water from the north to create dangerous currents and storms.

Grog.
Rum diluted with water, usually two parts water and one part rum. Grog could be diluted even further to minimize the effect of alcohol.

Hardtack.
A hard biscuit so resistant to spoilage that it could last several months. Unlike meat, other foodstuffs, and water that often did go bad, this flour and water cracker (baked with no salt) remained unaffected.

Helm.
The mechanism, and position taken by the ship's Captain, by which the ship was steered; it's connected to the rudder.

A re-creation of a ship's helm at the Mariners' Museum.

The rudder to a re-created ship at the Jamestown Settlement. (Pirates would usually immobilize the rudder to prevent the ship from being able to maneuver and make its escape.)

Holystone. Sailors scrubbed the decks of ship with this sandstone.

Keelhaul. Used to enforce discipline and act as a deterrent, this punishment involved tying the victim's ankles and wrists, throwing him overboard, and dragging him under the keel of the ship, until he was pulled out from the other side. Usually, the sharp barnacles would cut into his skin and often lead to often fatal infections—if he escaped any hungry sharks lurking below.

League. A unit of measure, approximately three miles.

Letter of marque. A license given by a government to privateers allowing them to attack enemy vessels.

Logbook. After estimating a ship's speed, readings are recorded in this book.

Longitude. The east-west orientation that could not be accurately determined until the invention of an accurate timekeeper in the eighteenth century. The fascinating story of longitude is chronicled in Dava Sobel's book of the same name.

Long shot. A gun firing round shot at a great distance rarely hit its intended target due to the inherent variables involved: inability to accurately adjust for elevation, no means to traverse (laterally, left and right), variations in powder, tube wear, round shot variations, etc. Since the likelihood of actually hitting the target under these circumstances was very problematic, it was correctly termed a low-probability shot—a long shot.

Man-O'-War. A warship, usually heavily armed.

Peg leg. A wooden leg, a prosthetic device.

Pieces of eight. Part of a Spanish silver coin used as a currency worldwide. The coin was cut into eight pieces, called pieces of eight, for small transactions. Pieces of eight are not to be confused with Spanish doubloons—gold coins.

Pillory. A form of punishment involving a wooden frame through which one's head and hands protrude.

The public stock in Colonial Williamsburg. (Blackbeard's pirates were on display before being transported to the "publick gaol.") The neck was put through the larger hole and the hands went through the smaller holes. This required the victim to be standing up and bent over—an uncomfortable position to hold for long periods of time, especially outdoors in inclement weather.

Pirate flags. Usually black, these were used to signify the true colors of the pirate vessel when she wanted to reveal herself and her true intentions. The presumption was that the enemy vessel would surrender without a fight. A red flag meant that the ship's pirate crew would neither ask nor give quarter—any mercy—and it was a fight to the finish.

A premeasured charge of gunpowder, on exhibit at the Mariners' Museum.

A close-up of a flintlock pistol on display at James Fort, Jamestown Settlement.

Pistol. A highly valuable and prized weapon among pirates, and deadly if fired at short range. Blackbeard, it was said, used silk ribbons to tie his pistols to himself, so he could fire a pistol, drop it, and pick up another one to continue the assault. Obviously, given the time required to reload a flintlock pistol, Blackbeard's ingenious solution was the best course of action.

Poop deck. Usually the highest deck on the ship, located at the stern (the rearmost area of the ship). The captain's quarters are usually located beneath it.

Quarter/no quarter. If a pirate ship met with no resistance, it usually gave quarter, meaning it did not harm the crew. No quarter, however, meant that it was a fight to the death, and neither side expected any mercy.

Rudder. At the aft part of the ship, it steers the ship. Pirates would often disable the rudder of the enemy ship before boarding to prevent it from maneuvering.

The steering mechanism for the rudder, on a re-created ship at the Jamestown Settlement.

Salmagundi. A particularly spicy soup that included anything available to enhance its flavor: meats, vegetables, spices, and fruits.

Schooner. Statistics show that this was the most popular form of vessel used by pirates. It was fast, highly maneuverable, and had a shallow draft, allowing it to maneuver in places larger ships couldn't. It could accommodate a crew of approximately seventy-five men and several guns, as well. According to David Cordingly, author of *Under the Black Flag,* a little over half of all pirate attacks were carried out in schooners.

Scuttlebutt. Gossip.

Sea shanty (chantey). A sea song, like "Yo ho, yo ho, a pirate's life for me!" which was sung by a preteen Elizabeth Swann in the opening scene of *Curse of the Black Pearl.* It was sometimes called a chantey.

Seven seas. The world's seven seas. To say you've sailed the seven seas means you've sailed all over the world. (Can you name all seven?)

Shot. The ammunition fired by ships' guns. Round shot—an iron ball of varying weight, depending on the size of the gun—was most common.

Shot used in shipboard guns, on display at the Mariners' Museum.

A swivel gun mounted on the starboard side of a
re-created ship at the Jamestown Settlement.

Swivel gun. Used by pirates to shoot a round past the bow of
an enemy ship in an attempt to get the crew to stand down and prepare to be boarded.

Conditions

Becalmed. A state in which a ship's sails were temporarily use-
less because the wind and water were calm.

Careen. To deliberately lay a ship on its side during low tide so
that maintenance could be done below the water line. Essential for
cleaning off barnacles and seaweed, which would slow a ship
down, and for getting rid of "ship worm," a parasite that damaged
the wood in the manner of termites.

Maroon. A form of punishment where the offender is deliberately abandoned on a remote island with the likelihood that sooner
(if by flintlock pistol) or later (if by starvation), he'd die.

Expressions

Black Jack. Slang for the pirate flag, the Jolly Roger.

Clap in irons. To use iron manacles for the wrists/legs to secure a prisoner. This was often done when the ship lacked a jail cell.

Dance the hempen jig. Pirates usually did not live long, healthy lives; they instead, usually lived short, unhealthy lives, often marked by this colorful phrase which meant, simply, hanging by the neck with a rope until dead. "Dancing" means the leg movements that characterized a man when he's dangling and kicking; hempen refers to the thick rope used. Note: If you're going to hang by the noose, it's best to be well-hung, as the pirates would say. You would hope the noose is properly knotted so that it'll choke you quickly, instead of simply having you dangle at the end of the looped rope, which needlessly prolongs the experience.

Davy Jones' locker. The bottom of the ocean, a watery grave.

Dead man's chest. Not an actual chest, as the second *Pirates of the Caribbean* movie suggests, but a reference to Dead Chest Island in the British Virgin Islands, a popular place to maroon a victim. Also, a coffin was commonly called a dead man's chest.

I'll see you measured for chains. A particularly nasty threat, one that was greatly feared by pirates. Before a pirate was hung, he'd be carefully measured. The measurements were taken so that after the hanging, he'd be hung out to dry: It normally took up to two years for the tarred body to fully decompose. Meanwhile, the body would be tightly held in the iron bands that encircled him. This was used as a warning to all other pirates, basically saying: "See what will happen to you if you're a pirate and we catch you!"

Kiss the gunner's daughter. Used by the Royal Navy, this meant whipping a man while tied over a gun's barrel. Another variation of this was called "Kissing the Wooden Lady" in which the man would wrap his arms around the mast, have his wrists tied, and then be whipped. Both were usually administered for minor offenses.

Let the cat out of the bag. Removing the cat-o'-nine-tails from its canvas bag to administer a whipping.

Rattle the bones. Shake those dice! Pirates were notorious gamblers, and playing cards and dice were some of their favorite pastimes.

Shiver me timbers! An expression that means, "I'm *really* surprised!" Timbers refers to the wooden planks on a ship, so to use this expression means that you are surprised to your very core.

Stay the course. A nautical term meaning that if a ship was headed in a specific direction and it didn't vary from that course, then it would arrive at its intended destination.

Sweating. A particularly vicious form of punishment in which you were forced to run around the ship until you dropped, egged on by pirates using cutlasses and other sharp objects as you made the rounds.

Sweet trade. The pirate profession.

Walking the plank. A punishment falsely associated with pirates; a board was set up to extend past the edge of the ship, and at gun or swordpoint, the victim would simply walk on the plank until he dropped off. There is, however, no evidence of pirates using this technique.

"We plead our bellies." Refers to pregnancy, which allowed female pirates to escape hanging because it was illegal to kill an unborn child.

2. HOW TO DRESS LIKE A PIRATE

Plunderwear and Pirattitude:
Clothing, Accessories, Weapons, and 'Tudes

Though movie studios are known to take literary license when interpreting history to suit a storyline, great care is taken to hire a designer who is responsible for what all the characters wear. No doubt about it: Clothes make the actor or the pirate. If you want to dress like a pirate, Chances are that unless you're chosen as a movie extra, you will need to find your own plunderwear. Fortunately, there's no lack of clothing, accessories, and weapons for swashbucklers and scalawags, or ladies and wenches, if you know where to look. Whether your interest is casual (a Halloween party, a pirate-themed party, or a cruise on a pirate ship) or serious (working as a reenactor or attending a pirate festival), to act the part, you have to look the part.

An 18-inch Jack Sparrow figurine from NECA, and a photo of Jack Sparrow signed by actor Johnny Depp ($450) at Sid Cahuenga's One-of-a-Kind Antiques and Curios at Walt Disney World Resort.

The existing *Pirates of the Caribbean* movies are a good reference point for what may suit you. In general, the movies have historically accurate costumes, with a few liberties taken. Historical reenactors have found fault with some of the costumes, but the general public is happy with what they saw. The fashion-conscious Governor Swann dresses for success and would rather be dead than be seen in anything less than the finest clothing that money and London tailors can provide. His daughter, Elizabeth Swann, prefers comfortable clothes to the finery of London fashion. But no matter what she's wearing—a gown or sailor's clothes—Elizabeth's a smart dresser. Will Turner can turn heads too, though he prefers to dress down, in working clothes. But when the occasion demands it—his wedding day—he can certainly dress the part. And Jack Sparrow is every inch the sartorially splendid pirate captain, with his tricorne hat, overcoat, and large black leather boots. As for the rest of his crew, well, they don't dress for success because they don't *have* to: They're pirates, after all.

According to Angus Konstam, in *Pirates 1660-1730,* "pirate captains frequently adopted the dress worn by successful merchants, giving the wearer the appearance of a gentleman. This meant wearing breeches, a waistcoat, and a long outer coat." In fact, says Konstam, historical records show that some pirates were even hung in all their finery, wearing "velvet jackets, breeches of taffeta, silk shirts and stockings, and fine felt tricornes."

A pirate crewmember, however, would have little need for finery. His wardrobe favored plain clothing, including a cap (to protect him from the relentless Caribbean sun), plain shirts, trousers, and a short jacket. In short, he wore functional clothes, since his ship duties required durable workaday clothing.

Similarly, female pirates favored utilitarian male clothing, not only to help blend in with the all-male crew but also because of its durability and wearing comfort.

The well-dressed woman in the eighteenth century was a slave to current fashion. This meant wearing elaborate dresses, gowns with a corset underneath, which Elizabeth Swann rightly cursed in *Curse of the Black Pearl*.

Pirates, though, rarely found themselves in the gentrified company; they were more likely to enjoy the company of working class women, who dressed for practicality, not visual effect.

As any character actor working at a theme park or a historical park like Colonial Williamsburg will tell you, clothes are not enough. You have to be the personage in question. Besides, what's the fun in being yourself when you are dressed up in period clothing? Don't you want to be someone else for a change? Think how boring it'd be for your friends to see you wearing pirate garb and talking and acting like the same old you that they know all too well. Guys, let the pirate clothes transform you from an ordinary specimen to a swashbuckling figure!

More than anything else, pirates were intimidating figures, so adopt the right persona: Be bold, be aggressive, and show your pirattitude! Strike fear into the hearts of ordinary citizens. Arm yourself to the teeth and exhibit your latent, aggressive nature!

N. C. Wyeth's pirate illustrations are excellent visual interpretations of how a pirate should act. His images of dagger-in-teeth pirates clearly suggest that these guys were given a wide berth—or else!

Now, as for interpretation, the *Pirates of the Caribbean* movies offer four models on which to base your pirate persona. Men have two diametrically opposed choices: Captain Jack Sparrow (good pirate) or Captain Hector Barbossa (bad pirate). For ladies there are no bad choices: Elizabeth Swann as the picture of English elegance and refinement, or Elizabeth Swann in male sailor garb. There are also Anamaria and Tia Dalma, but let's face it, they're not typical, are they?

The key point to remember is that if you are going to immerse yourself in the pirate experience (preferably at a pirate festival, a renaissance fair, a party, or a shipboard cruise), you have to think and act like your character; you have to live the part. Deep-six your own persona and transform yourself into someone else.

Captain Jack Sparrow:
The Archetypal Bad Boy, the Gonzo Pirate

If you want to be Jack, whose character was inspired by the infamous pirate Blackbeard, here's what you need to wear:

1. A bandana/head scarf, preferably red in color

2. Black makeup under the eyes to reduce the glare of the sea—it also makes the eyes stand out (just enough to accent, but not enough to make you look like a raccoon)

3. A full moustache

4. A beard with twisted ties (like Blackbeard)

5. Long dreadlocked hair with beads and trinkets in it (or a wig if you prefer)

6. A sea-worn, battered tricorne cap (Jack wears leather, but tricorne caps were made of felt)

Cover story for *Rolling Stone* on gonzo pirate Jack Sparrow as interpreted by actor Johnny Depp.

7. A heavy overcoat with flaring cuffs and a matching dark vest to go underneath

8. A loose-fitting, comfortable white shirt made of rough material for contrast against the dark coat—wear it open to display your hairy chest

9. A large leather belt (or two) as Jack wears in *Dead Man's Curse*

10. A knotted sash tied around the belt

11. Rings galore! Be a lord of the rings!

12. Heavy dark pants

13. Seaboots made of leather (perfect for concealing a pair of dirks, by the way)

14. A cutlass and a flintlock pistol as accessories

15. Plenty of tattoos, especially a "P" on the right forearm

16. Beaded wrist bands

17. A handheld compass that points "to the thing you want most in the world," as Jack Sparrow explained to Elizabeth Swann.

18. A tan (a self-tanning product like Tan in a Can is preferable to a cancer-inducing session under the sunlamps)

19. Dark, penetrating brown eyes (use contact lens to go brown)

20. At *least* three gold-capped teeth

To successfully pull off this look, however, you must supplement it with Jack Sparrow pirattitude:

1. Verbal circumlocution. When talking to your subordinates, use verbal word play as you would use your sword: fencing, parrying, and thrusting, but most of all, confusing your opponent so he doesn't know what to think and nods agreeably with your every pronouncement. (As Abraham Lincoln observed: Better to remain silent and be thought a

fool than to speak out and remove all doubt.)

2. Flirt shamelessly with beautiful women. This works best if you're tall, dark, handsome, rich, and famous.

3. Be able to think on your feet. Rely on your verbal skills to get you out of a tight fix, if your sword isn't enough to do the job.

Steven Dapcevich of The Pirate Empire as Captain Jack Sparrow.

4. Have some competency with a sword. Know how to thrust, parry, counterattack!

5. When sailing into port, look as if you are in command of your water-going vessel, no matter its size. This is the essence of pirattitude: Take command, for pity's sake, you're supposed to be a pirate!

6. Be a good negotiator. If you find yourself in over your head, or if you're confronted by a supernatural being who is clearly capable of killing you in painful and exquisite ways, be conciliatory and strive to strike a deal. Invoke said supernatural being's self-interest. Don't try to be a hero.

7. Above all, don't beg! There's no dignity in begging (or pleading), even for your miserable and worthless life, you scurvy dog! Keep in mind the young English boy in the remake of *Peter Pan* (2003). When confronted by Captain Hook, who offers to spare his life if he begs, the little boy screws his courage to the sticking place and retorts, "English gentlemen don't beg!"

8. Be funny or, better yet, be witty. This shows that you have a sense of humor. After all, pirating is not always about burning, pillaging, and destroying.

9. Don't be afraid to call a spade a spade. If accused of being a thief, liar, or cheat, simply point out the obvious and say, as Jack Sparrow does on several occasions, "I'm a pirate." Meaning, so what did you expect?

10. Have a philosophy you can live with that helps define your worldview. Jack says, "The only rules that really matter are these: what a man can do and what a man can't do." A workable philosophy is like a old shoe: It fits well and provides comfort and support.

11. Cut what deals you must, but always with your self-interest in mind. If you're in prison, get out of prison. If in a tough spot, get out of it. The best way to look after yourself is to make others agree to help you for just compensation.

12. When sword-fighting, fight verbally as well. Get your opponent to lose his temper, get flustered, and get distracted, which may affect his swordplay. When fighting another man, suggest he spends far too much time practicing sword-fighting because it's easier than winning a fair lady's heart. (This is termed the Jack Sparrow Feint.)

13. When dealing with the ladies, don't be shy. As the poets remind us, a faint heart never wins a fair lady.

Bottom line: If you want to pass yourself off as a convincing pirate, **BE A PIRATE.** Leave your real-world persona behind and step into large seaboots with which you can stride oceans.

Anything else? Yes. Slur your speech slightly to give the impression that you've had just a *bit* too much rum. Why come across as boringly sober? That's Will Turner's job. And be a bit of a dandy. Not enough to suggest anything untoward, but enough to show that you've got your own personal style.

Let's face it: no matter where Jack goes in the world, he's instantly recognizable by friend or foe, on land or at sea, because he's a one-of-a-kind, certified, dyed-in-the-wool, unapologetic character with his own sense of style. Norrington may think that

Jack Sparrow is the worst pirate he's ever heard of, but he *has* heard of him! At least 90 percent of the entries on online pirate message boards are about Johnny Depp in his role as Captain Jack Sparrow. As Depp remarked about Jack Sparrow: "He's me and I'm him. He's a character born out of me, but I don't trust him at all." He's a rogue, but a likable and (to the ladies) lovable one.

Left figure: Steven Dapcevich of The Pirate Empire as Captain Jack Sparrow on the deck of a ship at Mariners' Museum in Newport News, Virginia.

Captain Hector Barbossa:
The Archetypal Bad Guy

Note: This character was inspired by Captain Barbarossa, otherwise known as "Redbeard." The "look" is everything with this character. If you want to be the traditional bad-to-the-bone pirate, this is the character to dress like and emulate. For a color motif, think blue. To get Captain Barbossa's look you will need the following:

1. An outrageously large hat with blue ostrich feathers because you're a bit vain and wouldn't be caught dead without it, you popinjay!

2. Shoulder-length scraggly hair framing your ruggedly unhandsome face to show you really don't care how you look

3. A long moustache

4. A full beard

5. An ornate, full-length blue coat with large, buttoned cuffs made of silver

6. A colorful sash dangling from your belt

7. Black pants

8. Black boots

9. A chain with a mysterious pendant attached

10. Bad teeth (and at least one of them gold)

11. A large leather belt with ornate silver buckles

12. A fancy flintlock pistol

13. A cutlass

Now for the Barbossa pirattitude:

1. Be a very skilled swordsman.

2. Don't tell anyone your first name is Hector. What kind of name is *that* for a pirate?

3. Have a stern, penetrating stare. The key word here is intimidation.

4. Have a pet capuchin monkey perching on your shoulder. Name him Jack, after your favorite pirate.

5. Carry yourself as if you've been afflicted with a world-wearying ancient curse, an unending burden that weighs heavily on the mind and spirit.

6. Issue orders in simple, declarative sentences, so your crew will not mistake them.

7. Look stern and resolute. Be a captain good enough not only to command a ship, but also to command a ship of cursed dead pirates—the worst kind.

8. Make promises, but think like a lawyer. There's *always* a loophole you can take advantage of when negotiating, one that your opponent will not even consider.

9. Be polite to the ladies. Just because you're an undead pirate doesn't mean your manners should be coarse. Show some class.

10. Talk straight. Leave Jack Sparrow's verbal locutions and circumlocutions to the master.

11. Be a gentleman. Many ship captains dressed like gentlemen, so why not be a gentleman?

12. Be greedy for gold and other treasures. Stockpile them for a rainy day.

13. Long for the crunchy taste of apples. It's a small, personal thing, but it lends depth to your character.

14. When angry, show it—pirate passion.

15. Don't demand respect, command it. Earn it. Be the best and the rest will follow.

16. Always keep your options open and don't burn bridges behind you. You never know from whom you may need help, or when, as Elizabeth Swann, Will Turner, and Jack Sparrow soon learn.

Bottom line, then: Your type-A personality demands that you dress and act like the king of pirates. You are the archetypal pirate, capable of holding your own, in a profession that allows for democratic rule. When not in battle, your crew can vote you out of your command. So in order to keep your command, you need to be the biggest, baddest swashbuckler that ever plundered the seven seas.

Elizabeth Swann:
English Lady

The traditional look will no doubt appeal to a segment of ladies who attend pirate festivals. Like Elizabeth Swann's contemporaries who fit comfortably within the confines of both high society and corsets, some women today prefer the formal look with all its elegance, refinement, and respectability. It's a look that says, in no unmistakable terms, I'm a lady and I want to be treated as one. For such a person, dresses and gowns are the uniforms of the day. A fan is optional, but jewelry is not. No doubt a woman who shows up at a renaissance fair or pirate festival dressed in sartorial splendor will catch the eyes of peg-legged pirates and gentlemen alike. (It helps if you do your shopping at GypsyMoon.com.)

The other side of Elizabeth Swann is her tomboy nature. She's uncomfortable in the constraints of formal dress and customs and prefers the freedom of a white shirt, sailor's pants, and a short overcoat. It's this side of Elizabeth that we see the most in the *Pirates of the Caribbean* movies.

A stark contrast to the early Disney heroines in *Snow White and the Seven Dwarfs*, *Cinderella*, *Sleeping Beauty*, *The Little Mermaid*, *Aladdin*, and *Pocahontas*, Elizabeth Swann has a lot more in common with the heroine of *Mulan* and other films in which a young woman not only calls her own shots but also isn't afraid to take deadly aim with a pistol when the occasion calls for it. In other words, because Elizabeth Swann is very much a symbol of today's young woman, the only real decision is whether to dress for success (the classic look) or to dress for comfort.

In either event, here's how you ladies can properly pull off the role of Elizabeth Swann:

1. Submit, however uncomfortably, to the formal conventions of high society. But be prepared, as the situation dictates,

to throw all formality overboard and embrace your freer nature. Go pirate, in other words. Even in sailor's garb, Elizabeth can catch the male eye.

2. Have a lot of spunk. Don't be a shrinking violet.

3. Be your own woman, not an appendage in a marriage to a career man like Commodore Norrington. Being a dutiful wife is not in your cards. Besides, it's boring. Ask any military wife.

4. Be familiar enough with firearms to be able to use them if and when the occasion arises. And, to paraphrase Robert A. Heinlein, beware of strong drink, for it will make you aim at weasels like Lord Cutler Beckett . . . and miss.

5. Exhibit a fierce intelligence. You should be able to think, not fight, your way out of a problematic situation.

6. Be loyal to your true love: You either will . . . or will not.

7. Be able to think on your feet. Always invoke the right to parley if the situation demands it.

8. Be loyal, even if it means going to the ends of the Earth to do the right thing.

9. If all else fails, use your feminine charms. This is how Elizabeth Swann finally tricks Jack Sparrow, which proves to be his ultimate undoing. (Don't forget: A woman on board a ship will always bring bad luck.)

Sources for Clothing

On the presumption that you want to really look the part, I'm recommending some sources for period clothing rather than costumes. The distinction is that costumes are lower-end merchandise appropriate for Halloween or parties, while period clothing is authentic and priced accordingly. In most cases, your best bet is to buy a whole ensemble, though those of you with a taste for personal flair (like Jack Sparrow) will want to buy a la carte, to achieve just the right look.

1. Authentic Wardrobe (www.authenticwardrobe.com). Men's frock coat and pants ($695); shirt, vest, and hat ($395); baldric and gloves ($395); or the full ensemble ($1,295). Not cheap, but you'll certainly look the part. Boots and weapons not included.

2. Blackbeard's Creations (www.blackbeardscreations.com). Pirate rigs ($150) to hold your sword and other accessories.

3. Captain Jack's Pirate Hats (www.captjackspiratehats.com). From the website, "I present for ye the largest selection of Pirate headwear to be found on the High Seas. Here be the finest, authentic, handcrafted wool felt, sea grass, and straw pirate hats, with eleven standard styles of Cocked Hats from the golden age of piracy."

4. Painted Lady Crew (www.paintedladycrew.com). Clothing and accessories for men and women.

5. Silhouettes Clothing Company: Pirate Specialist (www.topnotchcostumes.com). An excellent selection here: coat, vest, pants, skirt, shirt, sash, headscarf, buttons, wig, pirate jewelry. They also offer (for those who want a complete outfit) two "Jack" packages: (a) "muslin shirt, Captain Jack pants, printed head scarf, two stands of pirate jewelry, three temporary tattoos, best Jack sash and wig" for $435. (b) "linen shirt, Captain Jack pants, new vest, wig, printed headscarf, replica jewelry (*not* sold separately), faux leather hat, best Jack sash, and three [hopefully temporary] tattoos" for $949.

6. Carlisles Historic Clothing (www.carlislesonline.com). A very good selection of doublets, shirts, breeches, hats, scarves, pirate garb, weapons, armor, and more.

For knockoffs of Elizabeth Swann's dresses, do an eBay search. There are dozens of merchants that sell pirate-related clothing of varying quality and prices. See the list of websites at the back of this book in the appendices, go to www.noquartergiven.net/merchant.htm, and click on "Costuming/Period Clothing," or do a Google search for "pirate costumes." Children and young adult-sized costumes can be found on numerous websites, including www.disneyshopping.com, anniescostumes.com, or buycostumes.com (to name a few).

Pirate reenactors at the Salem Pirate Faire (Salem, Massachusetts).

3. HOW TO FIND YOUR WAY AROUND A PIRATE SHIP

As with any profession, the nautical profession has its own vocabulary, which is understandably confusing to those who have never set foot on any kind of ship.

- ✪ Facing forward, the left side of the ship is called PORT.

- ✪ Facing forward, the right side of the ship is called STARBOARD.

- ✪ The ship's weapons are called GUNS. They are *not* called cannons.

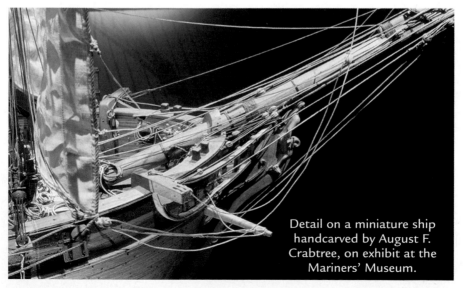

Detail on a miniature ship handcarved by August F. Crabtree, on exhibit at the Mariners' Museum.

Detail on a miniature ship handcarved by
August F. Crabtree, on exhibit at the Mariners' Museum.

- The guns protrude from GUNPORTS, the square/rectangular-shaped holes cut into the HULL of the ship. (When the guns aren't in use, the gunports are closed.) These guns can elevate but cannot traverse (from left to right).

- The front part of the ship is called FORE. (Think: forward.)

- The back part of the ship is called AFT. (Think: afterward.)

- The place where the food is cooked is called the GALLEY. It is not called the kitchen.

- The gun on a swivel mount is not called a cannon. It's called a SWIVEL GUN and was used to fire a warning shot across the bow of another ship, prior to boarding.

- The FLAG is located on the aft part of the ship. It's supposed to show the ship's nationality, but pirates often raised false colors initially and then its true colors, the Jolly Roger, when close enough to commence an attack.

- The CAPTAIN'S CABIN was located in the aft part of the ship on the main deck. An easy way to spot it was to look for the stern lantern.

- The area where most the shipboard activities took place is called the MAIN DECK.

- The KEEL of the ship is the "central fore-and-aft structural member in the bottom of a hull, extending from the stem to the sternpost and having the floors or frames attached to it usually at right angles: sometimes projecting from the bottom of the hull to provide stability" (from dictionary.com). This is not what a pirate cares to see when the ship is under way, since keelhauling was often a death sentence.

- The FORECASTLE is the crew's quarters, usually comprised of a large room in which hammocks can be strung.

An interior shot below deck of a replica ship moored at the Jamestown Settlement, Jamestown, Virginia.

A crow's nest on a miniature ship, on display at the Mariners' Museum.

❂ The HOLD is where the cargo is located.

❂ The HATCH is the entryway into the lower part of the ship, into the HOLD.

❂ The tall timber holding up the sails is called the MAST.

❂ The CROW'S-NEST is located near the top of the MAST, which allows visibility for up to twenty miles depending on atmospheric conditions.

❂ The BRIG is not the place to store prisoners; it is a vessel with two masts, used by pirates.

4. HOW TO LIVE LIKE A PIRATE: SEA CRUISES

If you had the opportunity to go on a pirate cruise on a replicated ship and live the life of a pirate, you would probably jump at the chance. Think about it: fresh sea air, freedom to do what you wish (you're a pirate, after all), lots of rum, and tropical ports of call where you can enjoy the spoils of your plunder and not have a care in the world. Sounds pretty good, doesn't it?

As young Elizabeth Swann says in *Curse of the Black Pearl*, from her vantage point on the deck of a British ship, "Yo ho, yo ho, a pirate's life for me. . . ." Chances are good, though, that if you were go on an authentically re-created cruise that mirrored a pirate's life onboard in every detail, you'd likely jump ship at the nearest opportunity. Let's look at what life would be like on a light French frigate like Blackbeard's ship, *Queen Anne's Revenge*.

Toilet Facilities

Forget modern facilities with a comfortable toilet seat, plumbing, and soft toilet paper. Instead, get used to walking to the front of the ship and sitting on a weather-worn (watch for splinters!) open seat with the ocean below. You'd have no privacy, a breezy feel "below deck," and depending on the weather, a seat that pitched forward or back or rolled from side to side. At night or in bad weather, you could do your business below deck on a primitive seat with pipe work that would duct out the ship. Think about what it'd be like to be in a constantly shifting outhouse, and you've got the idea.

Food

Food would not be a high point on an authentic pirate cruise. For one thing, there was no ice or refrigeration. As a result, most food and water eventually went bad. In fact, your choice of beverage would be fairly limited: wine, bad water, or more commonly grog (rum and water).

The selection of food is hardly appetizing. Although there are animals on board that can be slaughtered for meat (pigs, chickens, goats, sheep), and although fresh meat can be harvested from the sea (boiled sea turtles), most victuals were not chosen for their taste but for their ability to resist spoilage as long as possible. Meat, with its short shelf life, spoiled soon after the animal was slaughtered. A cracker called hardtack was properly named; it didn't spoil, but it had no taste and was hard as a rock. Its virtue was that it was somewhat filling if you ate enough of it.

Scurvy caused by vitamin C deficiency was a major problem. It wasn't until 1753 that James Lind, a Scottish naval surgeon, discovered the salutary effects of citrus fruits to prevent scurvy, which explains why oranges and limes became standard fare on ships. It's also why British sailors were called "limeys."

Sanitation

Barreled water, which went bad in warm climates because of algae growth, was precious and used for drinking and cooking only. For bathing, sailors took salt water baths. Lice were everywhere, in the clothes and in the bedding. It didn't help that animals were normally stored below deck, where pirates slept at night. The lice weren't the worst of it: Disease-carrying rats were everywhere. At the bottom of the ship, bilge water festered: a stench of human waste, animal waste, contaminated water, and foodstuff. The stench was indescribable, but pirates acclimated just as landlubbers who live downwind of slaughterhouses grow acclimated to their overpowering stench.

Living Conditions

Below deck, pirates found space to sleep wherever they could. It was crowded, dark, uncomfortable, and smelly. There was no privacy. Above deck, depending on the weather, it could be unbearably hot by day or cold at night, not to mention inclement weather and the occasional vexing hurricane.

Sleeping quarters beneath deck on a replica ship moored at the Jamestown Settlement, Jamestown, Virginia.

Maintenance

There's always plenty of work to do on a ship. Scrubbing the deck, repairing sails, running cannon crew drills, and fixing broken tools are just a few of the most obvious shipboard tasks. There were also long periods of intense boredom, somewhat relieved by card-playing or other diversions, punctuated by moments of stark terror: such is the nature of warfare, which has remained unchanged through the years.

Fear: An Occupational Hazard

There was also the ever-present concern of capture by a British force, which would almost always result in a trial quickly followed by a hanging. When the British ships went out to hunt down pirates, they went out well-organized, well-armed, and well-motivated. They usually did not return empty-handed.

In short, life onboard a pirate ship was hardly the romantic cruise it might seem to be. Fortunately for today's "pirates" who are accustomed to a higher standard of living, there are plenty of opportunities to pack up a kit bag and leave troubles behind by going on a modern cruise on a liner or a sailing ship. Costs vary considerably, but there's usually something for everyone, from children to adults, lasting from a few hours to week-long cruises.

Sea Cruises

Captain Memo's Original Pirate Cruise
(www.captmemo.com)

> Home port of call: *Clearwater Beach, Florida;*
> Propulsion: *twin diesel engines.*

The *Pirate's Ransom* is a custom-designed seventy-foot ship built in 1993 to Coast Guard requirements. It can carry 125 passengers. In addition to two-hour day cruises and sunset champagne cruises in the bay, it also hosts one-hour children's birthday party cruises and corporate and private charters. Its crew includes captains, wenches, and pirates, all with equally colorful names— Captain Memo, Panama Pam, Gangplank Gary, Shipwreck Sherri, and Bilgewater Bill, to name a few. There's no food available, but there are plenty of drinks on board (soft drinks or liquor). Afterward, be sure to take home a souvenir: A baseball cap or one of their black t-shirts would fit the bill.

Disney Vacation Cruises
(www.disneycruise.disney.go.com)

Home port of call: *Orlando, Florida, and*
Castaway Cay, Caribbean;
Propulsion: *engine.*

Although most people are aware that Disney's major US theme parks are in Anaheim, California (Disneyland), and Orlando, Florida (Walt Disney World Resort), few know that Disney has its own cruise line. This is the best way to experience the Caribbean for families with young kids. It's a little known fact that the *Flying Dutchman,* commanded by Davy Jones, is permanently moored in Castaway Cay; although you can't board it, you can rent a small boat and get near it to take pictures. According to Disney, the 175-foot long pirate ghost ship is "a prop from the hit film that appears to be destined to haunt the open seas for all eternity. Stay alert and you may catch a glimpse of the infamous Captain Jack Sparrow on the lookout for the commander of the *Flying Dutchman,* his new nemesis, Davy Jones."

Disney cruise ships include a Bahamian cruise and cruises to the Caribbean (eastern, western, southern). All cruises stop in Castaway Cay, which is owned by Disney. You can order a free vacation planning guide that will help you make an informed selection. It's on DVD and packed with a lot of information.

Jolly Roger Pirate Cruises
(www.funbarbados.com/Tours/jollyroger.cfm)

Home port of call: *Bridgetown, St. Michael, Barbados;*
Propulsion: *engine.*

A pirate party with pirate punch and plenty of barbecue.

Pirate Cruise from Annapolis
(www.baltimoretours.net)

> Home port of call: *Annapolis, Maryland;*
> Propulsion: *mechanical.*

Though billed as "a wonderful tour for families or kids of all ages," it's probably going to appeal more to children than adults. Unlike most of the other pirate cruises, Captain Billy "is portrayed by an anthropologist, historical interpreter, and musician who presents the character of the captain in 'first person' and in full eighteenth century garb. Musical instruments used during the performance correspond with instruments known during the colonial period." In other words, you get a ship captain that not only pilots the vessel but is in character for the duration of the ride.

Pirate Cruises of Bonaire
(www.remarkable.com/bonaire/pirates.html)

> Home port of call: *Bonaire; Netherlands Antilles;*
> Propulsion: *sail.*

The *Mistress* is a fifty-six-foot ketch (a sail ship with two masts). Various cruises are available, including one for kids (pizza is on the menu), one for watching dolphins (soda, wine, rum, and fresh fruit), one for watching turtles (snorkel gear included), and a dinner sail that boasts a seven-course dinner. This experience is recommended for those who want the authenticity of cruising on a ship under sail, not mechanical propulsion.

Plymouth Pirate Adventure
(www.lobstertalesinc.com)

Home port of call: *Plymouth, Massachusetts;*
Propulsion: *engine.*

Cruise on a forty-four-foot boat and help solve a mystery that leads you to hidden treasure and a lobster pot. Also charters short cruises for children aged four to eleven; each crewmember gets a pirate hat, treasure, candy, and his/her face painted, "and a boat load of fun."

Sea Dragon Pirate Cruise
(www.piratecruise.net)

Home port of call: *Panama City Beach, Florida;*
Propulsion: *engine.*

A two-hour cruise is available on this re-created, eighty-five-foot pirate ship, commanded by Captain Phil. Intended for the entire family, the activities include sword-fighting, firing the cannon, finding the treasure and sharing the loot, and keeping on the lookout for dolphins, seagulls, pelicans, and other marine life.

Whodunit Cruises
(www.whodunitcruises.com)

Ports of call: *various;*
Propulsion: *engine.*

Whodunit Productions and Royal Caribbean hosts pirate-themed, week-long mystery cruises. Budding actors out there should try the three day "Mystery on the High Seas" cruise. "When you board, you will be given a role to play for the weekend. Don't worry—if you are on the shy side, you can sit back and watch it all unfold. But if you are not, then you can use your character to find out as much as you can. The in-character actors will be mixing among you for the entire cruise."

Windjammer
(www.windjammer.com)

> **Ports of call:** *various throughout the Caribbean;* **Propulsion:** *sail.*

This company has four ships that sail in the Bahamas or the Caribbean. According to Laura Bly (*USA Today,* July 7, 2006), "As Johnny Depp's Captain Jack Sparrow would say: Arrrrr! . . . Mainstream cruise passengers may label it the Kmart of the Caribbean or camping afloat. But a tall ship voyage with Windjammer Barefoot Cruises is as close to a pirates of the Caribbean fantasy as a landlubber can get."

Adults can expect the following: so much rum, you'll feel groggy; a beauty contest for Miss Windjammer (shiver me timbers!); a scavenger hunt looking for, ah, unusual artifacts; and generous applications of essential sunscreen. In fact, these pirates are cheeky monkeys who delight in showing off their worst sides to those on a passing cruise ship.

5. How to Live the Life of a Pirate: Pirate Festivals

Once you talk the talk (speak like a pirate), walk the walk (find your sea legs and know your way around a ship), and show off the look (dress like a pirate), the next thing you'll want to do is *be* a pirate, if only for a day or a weekend. Pirate-related events are year-round and held around the US, especially on the east and west coasts. Let's talk about what specific events are held (when and where) and then talk about what to expect in terms of activities, displays, food available, and more. This list is not all inclusive. Check the pirate websites for updated information.

Keep in mind that pirate reenactors prefer to attend pirates-only events, especially at encampments, where they can really get in character and live the "sweet life." With that in mind, you may want to try a renaissance festival first, where folks are generally a lot more forgiving because pirates are usually a sideline event, relegated to a themed weekend. When you are very comfortable playing the role of a pirate, go to a full-blown pirate event where, if you're lucky, the public will mistakenly think you're part of the show.

Note: This listing includes nautical (tall ship) events and renaissance fairs, since they usually have a pirate component to them.
For current listings, check out www.thepiratesrealm.com and www.noquartergiven.net/calendar.htm.

January

The Gasparilla Pirate Fest
(www.gasparillapiratefest.com) Tampa, Florida

The *Jose Gasparilla,* billed as the "only full-rigged pirate ship," sails into the bay, escorted in by a flotilla of pleasure crafts. It docks at the Tampa Convention Center, where the mayor surrenders the Key to the City to the captain. A magnificent brunch is served at the Tampa Convention Center. A parade consisting of floats, marching bands, and pirates galore travels down a 3.5-mile parade route. A street festival in downtown Tampa features live entertainment, food, rides, games, and displays.

April

Lee Island Pirate Days Festival
(www.leepiratefest.com) Fort Myers, Florida

A family event that includes pirate ships with a sea battle, musicians, duels, reenactments, rides, games, and vendors selling all manner of crafts, goods, and food.

May

Isle of Eight Flags Shrimp Festival
(www.shrimpfestival.com) Fernandina Beach, Florida

So, what does it cost for admission? Well, a buck an ear. (Just kidding!) This one is for the whole family. The culinary focus is on Atlantic White shrimp, which is prepared and served up here to a crowd of 120,000 that has gathered annually since 1963. There's also a pirate invasion, a "Little Pirate" costume contest for kids, several concerts (rock, pop, jazz, and folk music), a fabulous art show that is one of the best outdoor art events in the US, and more seafood than anyone could possibly sample or eat.

June

Hampton Blackbeard Festival
(www.vasc.org/celebrationsbythesea) Hampton, Virginia

A great place to learn about Blackbeard, the most infamous pirate of them all. Be sure to get there early because this is a full day of piratical activities. I attended the 2006 festival in the company of my thirteen-year-old nephew Luke, who enjoyed himself thoroughly, as did I. The festival featured tours of several tall ships docked at the Hampton public pier, several pirate skits, a cannon salute, sea battles, the capture of Blackbeard's ship and

his head paraded in public (Blackbeard was beheaded by a British navy lieutenant), a trial of Blackbeard's crew (hang 'em high!), historical reenactments, a pirate duel, and vendors of every kind.

Now under the sponsorship of the Virginia Air and Space Museum, the annual Blackbeard Festival promises to be bigger, better, and bolder.

The infamous Blackbeard, on display at the Mariners' Museum.

Port Washington's Pirate Festival

(www.portpiratefestival.com) Port Washington, Wisconsin

Great fun for the whole family with pirate ship cruises, a pirate invasion, a pirate parade, a thieves' market, musicians, demonstrations, wandering entertainers, swordfights, a children's area, costume contests, and reenactors galore.

Cutthroats of Corona

(www.renaissanceinfo.com/pirate/index.html) Corona, California

According to the website, "The festival will cover the time period from 1660 to 1720. This includes buccaneers and the golden age of pirates. There will be hundreds of costumed pirates who have docked at 'Port Corona' for two weekends of revelry. There will be three stages of pirate entertainment, cannon demonstrations, pirate grub and grog, plenty of pirate booty to purchase, and a daily treasure hunt for the kids." In addition to crafts and goods for sale, there will be a "bride auction," pirates telling tales, treasure hunts, mock trials, a plunder auction, and reenactor/public encounters on the streets (as you'd find at Disney's theme parks).

Billy Bowlegs Pirate Festival

(www.fwbchamber.org/BillyBowlegs/index.html)
Fort Walton Beach, Florida

Named after eighteenth-century pirate William Augustus Bowles, the festival includes a pirate invasion, a pirate crew reveling in the streets, live music, plenty of food, arts and crafts for sale, and a children's area. Travel tip: Make sure you take the time to visit one of the city's most popular restaurants, the Black Pearl on Okaloosa Island, celebrated for its fine grub, including a mouth-watering, stomach-filling, appetite-satisfying, budget-friendly 6.5-ounce portion of lobster.

Big Bear Pirate Faire

(www.bigbearcityrenaissancefaire.com)
Big Bear, California

It's sponsored by the same folks who put on the Big Bear Renaissance Faire, so you can expect a well-run event for this new pirate faire. The centerpiece of the event is the *Time Bandit*, a re-creation of a pirate ship seen in the movie of the same name. There are treasure hunts, boats for sailing, ship-to-shore battle reenactments, battles on the court, court reenactments, stage shows, vendors, and, of course, lots of "sea" food: You see it, you want to eat it.

Charleston Maritime Festival

(www.charlestonmaritimefestival.com)
Charleston, South Carolina

As its name states, it's principally a maritime festival with marine exhibits, displays, a children's village, a fine art gallery, sailboat lessons, ship tours, a family boat building activity, workshops, music, spoon playing, dancing, cruises, and a BBQ feast.

Pirate Festival

(www.olcott-newfane.com/html/events.html)
Olcott Beach, New York

According to the website, "Musical entertainment, stage performances, food vendors, rides, a parade," and "other festival-related items centered on the pirate theme."

July

Pirate Invasion Weekend

(www.medievalfaire.com) Rock Creek, Ohio

Great Lakes Medieval Faire features a pirate-themed weekend ("Pirate Invasion") with a buccaneer's booty treasure hunt, a pirate show, a dinghy race, and a pirate costume contest.

August

Tall Ships Festival

(www.tallshipschannelislands.com) Oxnard, California

More of a maritime festival than a pirate's festival, but fun nonetheless for landlubbers who want to get a close look at sailing ships. This event has all the usual maritime activities: ship boardings, arts and crafts displays, wares for sale, commercial exhibitors, activities for kids, food, live music, reenactors, ship-to-ship battle reenactments, and a "pirates and swashbucklers" event.

Bill Johnston's Pirates Days

(www.alexbay.org) Alexandria Bay, New York

Can you believe it? This festival is ten days of pirate-related activities: magicians, magic shows, a block dance, treasure chests, a children's parade, children's boats, a children's magic show, a pirate invasion, juggling, balloon sculpting, pirate music, skits, buried treasure, raft races, cruises, "fight a pirate," a scavenger hunt, weapons demonstrations, and fireworks. Pirate heaven!

Fell's Point Privateer Day

(www.fellspointdevelopment.com/privateerday)
Baltimore, Maryland

Centered around a pirate theme, this festival has more activities than you can shake a cutlass at: magicians, pirate juggling, a pirate magic show, block dancing, create your own boat (for children), a pirate line-up (children), a pirate parade (children), a magic show (children), a pirate invasion of the town, pirate music, a pirate skit, a hunt for buried treasure, a raft race, a duck water-race (win $500 if your duck crosses the finish line first), a mini-gold tournament for little pirates (children), a little pirate cruise (children), a scavenger hunt for a gold coin, a weapons demonstration, a pirate skit, a balloon show, fireworks, a reptile exhibit, and much more.

The Pirate Festival at Historic Fort York

(www.thepiratefestival.com) Toronto, Ontario, Canada

The first Toronto Pirate Festival, held in 2006, had staged shows about the antics of Captain Savage and One-Eyed Katy, a musical group called Ceol Cara (translation, Musical Friends), a performance of Shakespeare's *The Merry Wives of York* by the Salty Cove Community Players, a pirate skirmish put on by Rogues in the Rigging, a musical performance by Two Roads Home, a one-man performance by Captain Thom Bedlam (his name says it all), a one-man show by the unbelievably adroit and multi-talented Long Jon Strong, a comic, unicyclist, juggler, renowned clown, circus instructor, master balloon sculptor, stiltsman, wire walker, equilibrist, actor, professional court jester and acrobat, a comedy skit by the Merry Wenches of Windsor, an audience participation skit called Men in Tights, a Middle Eastern dance ensemble (Arabesque Dance Company), and a performance on steel drums by Pirate Bosco. There was also an "adults only" night (ages 19 and over) billed as "A Night of Jolly Rogering"at the Thirsty Parrot Tavern. The host for the evening, Zoltan the Adequate Pirate, presented "Extreme Acts of Stupidity." He was joined by several special guests, surprises, beer, ale, wine, and a "band of scurvy dogs that put the 'Buck' in Buccaneer." It was an "evening of bawdy pirate drinking songs (blow me down!), buxom wenches (huzzah!), dangerous stunts (I can't look but I'll peek!), and enough laughter to fill your poop deck. Yo ho!

September

Meridian Festival

(www.meridianfest.com) Corona, California

Set in the fictional world of Meridian, live action role playing takes center stage. "Meridian is a live action event that will incorporate elements of Renaissance, Pirate Festivals, role playing, simulated battle, special effects, and fantastic costuming. Sort of like living and playing in a movie world." Sounds like a great way to immerse yourself in a fictional universe. Be sure to dress up for the occasion—your choice of a Ren Faire costume or a pirate costume.

Toshiba Tall Ships Festival

(http://tallshipsfestival.com) Dana Point Harbor, California

Billed as the largest annual gathering of tall ships on the West Coast, this festival has a host of nautical and pirate-related activities for the whole family. Separate admission is required for boarding the tall ships, but everything else—the activities, sea shanty concert, arts and craft shows, living history encampments, and vendor area—is free.

St. Louis Pirate Festival

(www.stlpiratefest.com) Wentzville, Missouri

Yo, ho, a pirate's life for thee! The St. Louis Pirate Festival has artisans and crafters, food, comedy, music, feats of derring-do, and enough ale to float a flotilla. "The craft Governor has invited pirates from all over the world to attend a festival in the capital city of Port Royal, where he plans to hand out letters of marque, papers legitimizing them as privateers. Such notorious buccaneers as Anne Bonny, Mary Read, Christopher Condent, and Black Bart have responded to this 'opportunity,' but a pirate is always open to opportunities, and a festival day abounds with them." Raise the sails and head to St. Louis!

Salem Pirate Festival

(www.pastimes1.com) Salem, Massachusetts

This company puts on several events, including a pirate event.

Pirate Invasion Weekend

(www.norcalrenfaire.org) Hollister, California

A renaissance faire with an interactive pirate-themed weekend. (Many of the costume photos in this book were taken at this event.) Fun for the whole family! Go there with your piratitude on!

Ojai Renaissance and Pirate Faire/ Gold Coast Pirate Faire

(www.goldcoastfestivals.com) Ventura, California

Billed as a "Renaissance faire with a pirate flair," its pirate village includes exhibits, demonstrations, treasure hunts, a parade, games, merchants' sell 'n plunder (vendors), food 'n grog, and live entertainment.

A pirate musical group, Captain Bogg and Salty
(courtesy of the Portland Pirate Festival).

Portland Pirate Festival

(www.portlandpiratefestival.com) Portland, Oregon

Prepare a boarding party, this one is worth your time! With historical reenactments, lots of pirate-themed music, a marauder's market, plenty of grub and grog, ship-to-shore battles, and the opportunity to board a privateer schooner, this event is for pirates of all ages. Bring plenty of doubloons because you'll need them.

Adventure Weekend: Seafaring, Pirates, and the Age of Exploration at the Maryland Rennaissance Festival

(www.rennfest.com) Crownsville, Maryland

One weekend of the Maryland Renaissance Festival is set aside for pirate-themed activities.

Howard Pyle Pirate Festival
(www.dnrec.state.de.us) Dover, Delaware

Turn-of-the-century illustrator Howard Pyle is the inspiration for this event, which features a pirate invasion, treasure hunts, costume contests, music, and food. The highlights of the 2006 event were talks on "Pirate Fact and Fiction" and "Howard Pyle: The Painter, the Pirates, and the Cape." Note: Many originals of pirate art by Pyle are on permanent display at the Delaware Art Museum in Wilmington. The museum is well worth a visit. Don't forget to take home a souvenir Pyle pirate print from the gift shop.

October

Loyal Order of Reenactment Enthusiasts: Workshops and Classes for Pirates
(www.noquartergiven.net) Corona, California

These workshops are put on by the experts in all things piratical. Obviously not a family event, it is a great experience for those who want insider knowledge of the pirate world. Like other reenactors, these folks take their work very seriously. They take great pride in their knowledge of every aspect of the "sweet trade." Note: If you were to buy everything you really need to look the part of a seaman, it'd cost you $1,600. Definitely not cheap but if you buy from their recommended sources, you'd fit right in on the deck of a seventeenth century ship.

Pirates of the Intracoastal
(www.boyntonfaires.com) Boynton Beach, Florida

During this event, the Intracoastal Park is transformed into Port Royal. "You will meet, interact with, and be entertained by historical characters . . . spend the day exploring this enchanted village, filled with skilled artisans who are happy to show you just how they keep the old ways alive with their beautiful crafts." Note: The parent organization also puts on a Medieval Faire in December.

Annual Buccaneer Days at Two Harbors

(www.catalina.com) Catalina Island, California

"For that little bit of Pirate in each of us, join the Buccaneers . . . for a great day of fun. Join us at the Paradise Carnival Cove for fun games and activities for all ages. Don your best pirate attire for the costume contest. Enjoy great food and dance the night away."

Invasion of the Pirates Flotilla

(www.wilmington-docks.com) Wilmington, North Carolina

See a flotilla of ships, a pirate invasion, a treasure hunt, and other pirate-related activities.

November

Florida Pirate Festival

(www.piratefair.com) Clearwater, Florida

Avast! A fun-filled weekend festival for the whole family. As *Coastal Living* magazine tells it, "Ahoy, mateys! Drop yer anchors at Coachman Park and bring yer bounty, cause the cutthroats be comin' and a mutiny is at hand. Party with pirate crews from all over the state at the third annual event, which features a dozen stage acts with magic, music, and comedy; heated battles; dining with the magistrate; unbelievable fire shows; treasure hunts; pirate ship adventure cruises; and more. Bring the little ones, as the fun-filled and family-friendly event abounds with activities for the smallest of first mates."

Pirates in Paradise Festival

(www.piratesinparadise.com) Key West, Florida

As Kenny Banya from *Seinfeld* would say, "The best, Jerry, the best!" This is the pirate event of the year, bar none, and only a bilge rat would disagree. This one has got it all: tall ships, pirate ships, a pirate attack on a fort, a thieves' market, a living history encampment, a historical reenactment of the pirate trials of Anne Bonny and Mary Read, a pirate's tavern flowing with ale and other alcoholic beverages, a pirate-themed art show, round-the-clock parties, a buffet with enough food to feed a shipload of starving pirates, talks by historians and writers, and much more. A "don't miss" event, this is the real deal for pirate fans.

Note: While you're in Key West, stop in at the world's best pirate museum, Pat Croce's Pirate Soul. While you're there, buy his book, Pirate Soul— *the best souvenir you could take away from the experience.*

St. Andrews Fall Seafood and Pirate Fest

(www.emeraldcoastevents.com)
Panama City Beach, Florida

"A seafood festival with a pirate twist along the bay in the historic St. Andrews area of Panama City at Carl Gray Park." It has entertainment and activities for kids, midway games and rides, arts and crafts from all over the country, round-the-clock entertainment, a pirate encampment, world-class pirate bands, and plenty of pirates roving the grounds interacting with the crowd.

Pirates Week Festival

(www.piratesweekfestival.com) Grand Cayman, Cayman Islands

Pirates Week has "music, street dances, costumes, games, food and drink, pirate invasion, kid's day, a glittering parade, sports events, Heritage Days, and fireworks."

A movie prop from *Pirates of the Caribbean: Dead Man's Chest,* on exhibit at the Disney Gallery in New Orleans Square, Disneyland Park, Anaheim, California. This prop is Davy Jones's Chest in which his beating heart resides.

A treasure chest display at the Pirates of the Caribbean gift store, seen when exiting the ride at Disney's Magic Kingdom in Orlando, Florida.

6. DISCOVER PIRATE HISTORY: MUSEUMS

A marooned pirate on display
at the Mariners' Museum.

A comprehensive listing of pirate-themed or nautical museums worldwide is beyond the scope of this book. For more information on US museums, consult the online directory at www.maritimemu seums.net, compiled by Robert Smith. He's also the author of *Smith's Guide to Maritime Museums of North America*, which covers more than 620 maritime, lighthouse, and canal lock museums.

Australian National Maritime Museum
(www.anmm.gov.au) Sydney, Australia

An outstanding nautical museum with an interactive website. A kids exhibit called "Here be Pirates!" that ran through February 2007 was described as follows: "Cut loose your cutlass and enter the world of pirates in a rollicking kids' adventure land. Storm a galleon, fire a cannon, and walk the plank. Crawl through a looter's lair in search of treasure, check your weight in gold, and practice your pirate patter. Can you tell a scimitar from a sitar? Can you crack the clues to the hidden hoard? You'll meet the ghastly ghost of Blackbeard and the motliest crew of swaggering seafarers you'd ever want to set eyes on." If Australia is a wee bit far away geographically, take a virtual tour of some of their current and permanent exhibits from the website.

Brandywine River Museum
(www.brandywinemuseum.org) Chadds Ford, Pennsylvania

The work of Howard Pyle's most famous student, N. C. Wyeth, a well-known and popular illustrator, can be seen at this museum. The museum celebrates the Wyeth tradition that began with its patriarch, N. C. Wyeth. His son Andrew Wyeth and grandson Jamie Wyeth are also celebrated in their own right, as are other members of the Wyeth family, a dynasty of American artists. N. C. Wyeth paintings on display include pieces from *Treasure Island, Kidnapped, The Black Arrow, The Boy's King Arthur, The Last of the Mohicans,* and other Scribner classics. Several posters are available of his work, but the one most pirate fans will want is the cover to *Treasure Island,* frequently reproduced in pirate books.

Colonial Williamsburg
(www.history.org) Williamsburg, Virginia

The only living museum of its kind, Colonial Williamsburg is a must for anyone who wants to get a feel for what life was like in the seventeenth and eighteenth centuries. Because it's a living museum, you can see reenactors in costume and in character. The blacksmith, the cooper, the shoemaker, and others are creating their handmade goods the old-fashioned way, with tools appropriate to the time.

A street sign outside the leather shop (saddlemaker) at Colonial Williamsburg.

The Colonial Williamsburg website is extensive, interactive, and has a wealth of information. Go there first and look around, and then make plans to visit Colonial Williamsburg in person. (SEE ALSO: Jamestown Settlement.)

Delaware Art Museum

(www.delart.org) Wilmington, Delaware

This museum is a must-visit destination for anyone with even a passing interest in the pirate artwork of Howard Pyle and his students, including N. C. Wyeth. Most people have only seen poorly printed reproductions of Pyle's art from *The Book of Pirates* and Wyeth's art from *Treasure Island*. This is a pity since the originals are breathtaking. The museum gift shop has high quality, inexpensive prints of Pyle's art, including some of his most famous and best-loved works of pirate art, including *Marooned, The Mermaid, So the Treasure Was Divided, Captain Kidd, The Flying Dutchman, Attack on a Galleon* (often seen as a book cover on pirate books), and *The Coming Tide*.

Expedition Whydah

(www.whydah.com) Provincetown, Massachusetts

According to its website, the *Whydah* is the only authenticated pirate shipwreck ever discovered.

Originally built in London for the slave trade, [the *Whydah*] was captured in the Bahamas by the famed eighteenth century pirate commander, Sam Bellamy, with an extraordinarily rich cargo aboard. Bellamy converted the eighteen-gun slaver to a pirate's flagship and took her on a raiding voyage up the Atlantic seaboard. As legend has it, Bellamy was returning to Cape Cod to rendezvous with his sweetheart, but history records that he met death instead when the *Whydah* was wrecked in an epic storm off Cape Cod on April 26, 1717.

The recovery effort has yielded a treasure trove of artifacts—200,000 at last count. (SEE ALSO: www.shipwreckcenter.org.)

Graveyard of the Atlantic
(www.graveyardoftheatlantic.com)
Hatteras, North Carolina

This museum is dedicated to the preservation, advancement, and presentation of the maritime history and shipwrecks of North Carolina's Outer Banks, which "entomb thousands of vessels and countless mariners who lost a desperate struggle against the forces of war, piracy, and nature. The Graveyard of the Atlantic, with one of the highest densities of shipwrecks in the world, holds some of America's most important maritime history."

Independence Seaport Museum
(www.phillyseaport.org) Philadelphia, Pennsylvania

This museum showcases nautical exhibits, maintains a nautical repository housing for "more than 12,000 volumes, 9,000 ship plans, and a significant collection of rare books, manuscripts, photographs, maps, and charts, and conducts two self-guided tours of the cruiser *Olympia* and the submarine *Becuna*."

Jamestown Settlement

(www.historyisfun.org) Jamestown, Virginia

At the Jamestown Settlement near Colonial Williamsburg, you can board three replicas of ships that sailed from England to Virginia in 1607: the *Discovery, the Susan Constant,* and the New Replica *Godspeed* (built in 2005 to herald the 400th anniversary of Jamestown Settlement). According to this official website, "visitors can learn about the four-and-a-half month voyage from England and take part in periodic demonstrations of seventeenth century piloting and navigation."

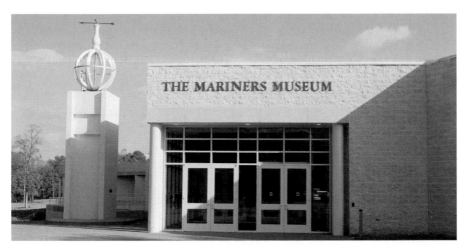

The entrance to the Mariners' Museum, Newport News, Virginia.

Mariners' Museum

(www.mariner.org) Newport News, Virginia

There are hundreds of nautical museums in the US, but for my money, the best one is the Mariners' Museum, which mounted a hugely popular 2006 exhibit, "Swashbuckler: The Romance of the Pirate," celebrating the popular-culture interpretations of the golden age of piracy with real-world pirate artifacts. With its vast collection of resources for students and journalists, its current and traveling exhibitions, and its impressive permanent collections, Mariners'

Museum has a staggering amount of nautical information and arti-facts. My personal favorites from the Mariners' Museum collections include the scientific instrument collection, which documents the art of navigation from the late fifteen to nineteen hundreds; the miniature ships of August F. Crabtree (astonishingly detailed, handmade mod-els); and "Exploration through the Ages." I suggest that you stop first at Mariners' Museum and then visit the living museums of Colonial Williamsburg and Jamestown Settlement thirty miles northwest.

Maritime Museum of the Atlantic
(museum.gov.ns.ca/mma/index.html)
Halifax, Nova Scotia

A part of the Nova Scotia Museum (a family of twenty-seven museums), the Maritime Museum's mandate: "to create for all an awareness, appreciation, and understanding of Nova Scotia's marine heritage through collection, preservation, research, interpre-tation, and exhibition." The collection includes "artifacts, images, charts, and plans relating to the marine history of Nova Scotia. The Royal Canadian Navy, Canadian merchant marine, Nova Scotia small craft, and local shipwrecks are particular strengths of the col-lection, much of which represent the period 1850 to the present. The collection includes everything from sextants, binnacles, and fig-ureheads to small crafts, anchors, armaments, marine portraits, and our largest artifact, the 1913 hydrographic vessel CSS *Acadia*."

Mystic Seaport: The Museum of America and the Sea
(www.mysticseaport.org) Mystic, Connecticut

"Mystic Seaport is home to one of the most important collections in the nation, including some 75,000 objects, 500 watercraft, over a million feet of film, all of which tell the fascinating story of America

A portrait of cartographers,
at the Mariners' Museum.

and the Sea." It also has "one of the largest, finest, and most thoroughly cataloged and thus accessible collections of maritime research material in the nation, housing many thousands of volumes, periodicals, manuscripts, logbooks, and ship plans." The museum has a wide range of programs scheduled year-round, including a program in October called "Nautical Nightmares: Maritime Ghost Stories" at which you will hear "tales of New England's historic ghosts, legends, and unsolved mysteries. Haunt historic vessels and exhibits, and hear spooky stories of lighthouses and ghost ships."

The National Maritime Museum and Royal Observatory
(www.nmm.ac.uk/site/navid/005) Greenwich, London

One of the finest museums of its kind in the world, its collection of material on Britain at sea is unparalleled. The collection contains "over two million objects related to seafaring navigation,

astronomy, and measuring time." The museum is currently in the process of putting as much as possible online. Its Maritime Art Greenwich is a learning resource with an extensive collection of art, viewable online. Make the time and stop by this world-class museum, in person or online.

A working hourglass on a replicated ship at the Jamestown Settlement.

The New England Pirate Museum

(www.piratemuseum.com) Salem, Massachusetts

From the website: "The tour starts in our artifacts room with authentic pirate treasures. Then you'll stroll through a colonial seaport, board a pirate ship, and explore an eighty-foot cave where you are sure to encounter some of the seventeenth century rascals face-to-face." The tour lasts approximately thirty minutes. When in town, you might also check out the Witch Dungeon Museum and Witch History Museum.

North Carolina Maritime Museum

(www.ah.dcr.state.nc.us) Beaufort, North Carolina

A great place to get your feet wet, because it's an excellent nautical museum in its own right. The real prize, however, is the recovery effort to bring artifacts from Blackbeard's flagship, *Queen Anne's Revenge,* that has resulted in numerous artifacts now on display. Well worth a trip to learn more about the most famous pirate of all time, Edward "Blackbeard" Teach.

Pirates Museum

(www.pirates-of-nassau.com/museum.htm) Nassau, Bahamas

Board a replica of the pirate ship *Revenge*; explore below deck to see its swinging hammocks, stowed cannon, volatile gambling sessions, and on board surgery under the ship's carpenter. Come face-to-face with female pirates Anne Bonny and Mary Read. See a three-dimensional re-creation of Howard Pyle's famous *Marooned* painting. Find yourself on an embattled ship as Blackbeard attacks and boards your ship. Watch a presentation that separates fiction from the facts of pirate life. See Captain Woodes Rogers confronting Hornigold. Witness the trials, hangings, and escapes of the era's most infamous pirates. Examine real pirate objects including cutlasses, flintlock pistols, and other memorabilia. A gift shop offers a wide selection of memorabilia—you really must buy something to take home!—and then go slake your thirst and put on the feedbag at its Pirate's Pub, a former brewery and guesthouse where you can enjoy international beers, tropical drinks, and their famous Pirate Punch. Food includes steaks, burgers, chicken, and fish.

Pirate Soul

(www.piratesoul.com) Key West, Florida

Welcome to pirate heaven. An American treasure, Pirate Soul is probably the best pirate museum in the world from one of the biggest pirate fans ever, Pat Croce, the author of *Pirate Soul*. According to its website,

> Pirate Soul Museum is a unique collection of authentic pirate artifacts coupled with elements of interactive technology revealing a historic adventure through the golden age of piracy and the lives of the era's most infamous pirates. With the "please touch" and audio-animatronics of a theme park coupled with the provenance of a museum, guests undertake an awesome pirate journey—both above and below deck—filled with compelling lore, surprising fact, and an abundance of sensory perceptions. Among almost 500 museum-quality artifacts, threaded through the storyline will be the original journey of Captain Kidd's last voyage, the only authentic pirate treasure chest in America originally belonging to Captain Thomas Tew, and Blackbeard's original blunderbuss.

If you only go to one pirate museum, make it this one. Furthermore, take the opportunity to visit Pat Croce's pirate-themed bar and restaurant, the Rum Barrel, for "great grub and grog" that includes conch fritters, coconut shrimp, grouper sandwich, succulent turkey legs, a traditional pirate stew, burgers, salads, and—to wash it all down—one of their 100+ rum drinks.

San Diego Maritime Museum
(www.sdmaritime.com) San Diego, California

Its mission is to *boldly go* where no man . . . oops, wrong ship, wrong century. "The mission of the Maritime Museum is to serve as the community memory of our seafaring experience by collecting, preserving, and presenting our rich maritime heritage and historic connections with the Pacific world." The museum holds "one of the world's finest collections of historic ships," hosts permanent and temporary exhibits on maritime history (including "Pirates of the Pacific"), stages public events such as family sleepovers on the *Star of India* (the world's oldest active ship), sails the *Californian* both in the San Diego Bay and to Catalina, and maintains the MacMullen Library and Research Archives for members, scholars, and researchers. Movie fans will undoubtedly want to see the HMS *Surprise,* a replica of an eighteenth century Royal Navy frigate featured in the film *Master and Commander: The Far Side of the World,* starring Russell Crowe as Captain Jack Aubrey from the Patrick O'Brian seafaring novels.

A display of Pirates of the Caribbean t-shirts at The World of Disney, Disney's flagship store in Orlando, Florida.

7. WALT DISNEY'S
PIRATES OF THE CARIBBEAN

Can you imagine going to a Disney theme park and seeing a static display of pirates through the ages billed as "Pirates of the Caribbean"? I can't and neither can you. Fortunately, Disney changed course and set sail in a new direction: Viewers witness a pirate attack on a seaport, which comes alive through patented Disney magic, called Audio-Animatronics®.

The resulting ride, which debuted in 1967 at Disneyland in California, proved to be a crowd pleaser. In fact, the ride was such a huge success that Disney installed the ride at the Walt Disney World Resort and at two of its theme parks overseas in Tokyo and Paris. It's considered an "E-ticket" ride, which is Disneyspeak for "one of the best experiences you'll ever have at our theme park." Each pirate cruise carries 3,000 people, which means that 500 million people worldwide have set "sail with the wildest crew that ever sacked the Spanish Main," as a Disney poster proclaims.

Disney has long profited from attractions based on popular movies. Now they are turning this model around, and profiting from movies based on popular rides. Like most film studios, Disney's interest in releasing stand-alone movies is a distant second to creating a film franchise where film after film can be released, set in the same fictional universe. George Lucas' space fantasy *Star Wars* made it clear that a well-conceived and popular film franchise is a cash cow. However, Disney had difficulty creating a successful film franchise of its own. Because of its poor history with fantasy films, Disney

The costume worn by actor MacKenzie Crook as the pirate Ragetti in the *Pirates of the Caribbean* films, on exhibit at the Disney Gallery in New Orleans Square, Disneyland Park, Anaheim, California.

studios passed on both Peter Jackson's *The Lord of the Rings* franchise and the Harry Potter series, thereby missing the boat on the two biggest film franchises of our time. Disney partnered with Walden Media to acquire the C. S. Lewis film franchise and found initial success with *The Chronicles of Narnia: The Lion, the Witch, and the Wardrobe*. (*Prince Caspian* follows in 2008.)

Instead of licensing expensive rights, Disney began looking within the company to find properties it could utilize to create the next film dynasty. The results of Disney's search within itself have been mixed. Three films (so far) have been made based on their most popular theme park attractions. Their first attempt, *The*

Country Bears (2003), proved to be a financial and critical disappointment. The Haunted Mansion was the next ride to make the transition from theme park to the theater. A necessarily dark film, *The Haunted Mansion* (2003) starring Eddie Murphy, grossed $75 million in the US. While considered a moderate success, *The Haunted Mansion* was not strong enough to justify box office sequels. Disney struck buried treasure on the third.

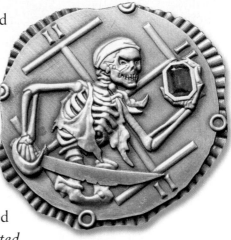

A pin design from Disney's extensive *Pirates of the Caribbean* pin collection.

The third ride-based movie *Pirates of The Caribbean: The Curse of the Black Pearl* (2003) proved to be a runaway success, grossing approximately $654 million worldwide. *Pirates of the Caribbean* was *the* ticket to ride. The film was just exactly what the public, long-tired of the depressing daily news about the second Iraq war, needed: a movie with pure escapism, a Saturday matinee with thrills, chills, and spills. In short, it was an Indiana Jones-type movie for the whole family, a popcorn movie; check your brain at the door.

The cast of characters includes a handsome and resolute hero, William Turner (played by heartthrob and former elf-warrior Orlando Bloom); a beautiful, spirited English girl, the Governor's daughter, Elizabeth Swann (played by the lovely Keira Knightley); an evil pirate named Captain Barbossa (delightfully played by Geoffrey Rush); a whole host of other cutthroats with cutlasses, ladies (both prim and not-so-prim), and a trained dog, to boot. But these are essentially stock characters that, in terms of megawatt appeal, cannot hope to match the most outrageous (in every sense of the word) pirate ever created, Captain Jack Sparrow, interpreted by one of the most outrageous (again, in every sense of the word) actors in our time, Johnny Depp, whose quirky roles had earned him fame but no fortune—until now.

Though there's much to praise in the films, the fact remains that the key selling point is Johnny Depp's masterful performance as the word-twisting, backstabbing, speech-slurring Captain Jack Sparrow. A gonzo pirate, Jack is a charming rogue, a colorful and engaging character who comes alive on the screen because of Depp's idiosyncratic performance. Depp was always ready to up the ante a bit—to go closer to the edge and peer over—to the initial dismay of Disney executives who felt he was over the top during early screenings. As it turns out, that was *exactly* what his character requires.

As the box office numbers and reviews came in, it was clear that Disney had finally found the proverbial treasure chest: "X" did indeed mark the spot, and the spot was *Pirates of the Caribbean*.

A box office and merchandising bonanza, *Pirates of the Caribbean* would set sail with two more sea ventures: *Dead Man's Chest* (2006) and *At World's End* (2007), filmed back-to-back.

The success also meant it was time to refurbish and update the Pirates of the Caribbean theme park rides, since it's well nigh unthinkable that there would be a ride without Jack Sparrow present. So Jack's back, not only in the film versions, but also on the classic ride. (Captain Barbossa is also on board the refurbished ride, as is Davy Jones.)

For an authoritative look at the Disney theme park ride and the film series it spawned, check out Jason Surrell's authorized book, *Pirates of the Caribbean: From the Magic Kingdom to the Movies*. Jason has done his homework and it shows. I can't think of any question about the theme park attraction that this book doesn't answer. It is a large, oversized book printed in full color on glossy stock that picks up every nuance of the numerous color reproductions and photographs—144 pages of pure Disney delight.

A *Pirates of the Caribbean* display at the World of Disney,
its flagship retail store in Downtown Disney (Orlando, Florida).

The Pirates of the Caribbean Theme Park Ride

Of course, there's no substitute for the ride itself, which can be enjoyed at Disney theme parks worldwide. As a repeat visitor to both Walt Disney World Resort and Disneyland, where I've ridden Pirates of the Caribbean several times, I prefer Disney World in Florida only because the park itself is bigger and there are more things to do.

Originally conceived as a static display of pirates throughout history, Pirates of the Caribbean made its impressive debut on March 18, 1967 in Disneyland as an elaborate audio-animatronic presentation with pirates sacking a Caribbean town. Since then, the ride has migrated all over the world to Disney's theme parks in Florida (Walt Disney World Resort), in Japan (Tokyo Disney Resort), and Europe (Disneyland Resort Paris).

A classic ride, it's been updated to reflect the Pirates of the Caribbean movies, with Jack Sparrow, Hector Barbossa, and Davy Jones making their first appearances. The boat ride lasts just under nine minutes, and the darkened world through which the ride travels heightens the anticipation. "Dead men tell no tales," an eerie voice intones, and it's hard not to believe it as the ride initially takes you through a stygian tunnel with a "curtain" on which Davy Jones is projected, as you hear music from the soundtrack come up.

The boat then plunges down a short drop, eliciting screams from the unsuspecting, as it travels through a darkened tunnel followed by a second unexpected drop that elicits more screams.

As the boat emerges, you are in the middle of a pitched battle as Captain Barbossa, commanding the *Wicked Wench*, urges his crew on. Sounds of the ship's guns, shouts and screams from the civilians in flight, and pirates urging each other on—it all combines to create a phantasmagoric effect, enhanced by the darkness and a city in flames. Pirates are running amok, ransacking the town at will.

We see our favorite tableaus—the pirates behind prison bars

reaching out in vain to a dog with keys in its mouth, and several young ladies being auctioned off, including a cheeky redhead who is warned by the auctioneer not to show off her impressive "super-structure." We also see Jack Sparrow, who takes refuge inside a barrel but emerges just long enough to see what's going on. Later, we see Jack lounging in a ship's cabin, surrounded by piles of gold and other treasures, so he's obviously come out on top—doesn't he have the luck of the devil?

As with all Disney rides, this one empties out into an appropriately themed gift store which is laden with more booty than you can shake

The costume worn by actor Lee Arenberg as the pirate Pintel in the *Pirates of the Caribbean* films, on exhibit at the Disney Gallery in New Orleans Square, Disneyland Park, Anaheim, California.

a cutlass at. Pirate merchandise unique to this store makes this an essential stop for anyone who wants to bring home a unique souvenir.

As *The Unofficial Guide to Walt Disney World* puts it, this ride is "Disney audio-animatronics at its best; not to be missed," earning a rare but wholly deserved five-star rating.

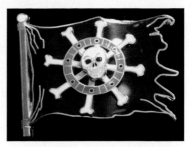

A pin design from Disney's extensive *Pirates of the Caribbean* pin collection.

Ye have been warned, me matey, pass on this ride at your own black pearl . . . er, peril!

Short Takes on the Films

Curse of the Black Pearl

Scott Warren (*Premiere* magazine): "*Pirates* is Indiana Jones on the high seas, complete with serial B-movie concept, wall-to-wall action, and fantastic myths come true."

Lisa Schwarzbaum (*Entertainment Weekly*): "Navigating by the trade route mapped out for [this movie], I reckon we've drifted into the Bermuda Triangle of the summer season, where movies disappear in front of our very eyes. Dead men tell no tales, the sea chantey goes, but neither will ticket buyers after sitting through this F/X-rattling Disney feature. . . ."

Dawn Taylor (*Portland Tribune*): "As a whole, *Pirates* is the rare case of an adventure movie where they got everything right. The plot—about mistaken identity and evil pirates trying to undo the effects of a cursed treasure—is complicated, but never falls apart. The art direction is superb, from the massive galleons and watery pirate caves to the computer-generated skeletal corsairs. The film's tone is dead-on, obviously made with the same sheer love for genre films that marks the best modern adventure movies, including *Raiders of the Lost Ark* and *Star Wars*."

Dead Man's Chest

Released on July 7, 2006, *Dead Man's Chest* proved the success of the first film was no fluke. The convoluted story, however, and the introduction of numerous supernatural elements took a toll on the reviews. As my thirteen-year-old nephew Luke observed, "It didn't seem as real to me as the first movie," meaning the excess of supernatural elements (Davy Jones, his crew, and the kraken) detracted from, rather than enhanced, the movie.

I think Luke's assessment summarizes what a number of critics felt: A weaker story line was buttressed by lots of computer-generated eye candy (including a lengthy and improbable sword fight scene involving a large mill wheel) and as much screen time as possible for Jack Sparrow, who not only saves the day but this film franchise, as well.

Let the critics walk the plank! The film went on to gross more than $1 billion worldwide. While some critics found much to like in the film, the ones who disliked it made no bones about their beefs. Bruce Westbrook (*Houston Chronicle*) took a few hard swings with his cutlass at the flick.

> Emboldened by the original film's $653 million global take, producer Jerry Bruckheimer has made a monster, turning a fun, fresh romp into a misguided mishmash of special-effects excess and horror-show repellency. The charismatic cast that sparked the original is lost in a tempest of supernatural meanies and repulsive creepiness.

If Westbrook took a few swings, Lisa Schwarzbaum (*Entertainment Weekly*) gleefully hacked away until she drew blood:

> Yes, indeed, *Pirates* 2.0 is a theme ride, if by ride you mean a hellish contraption into which a ticket holder is strapped, overstimulated but unsatisfied, and unable to disengage until the operator presses the restraining harness. . . . *Dead Man's Chest* cranks for what feels like an infernal eternity.

Disney's sequelitis problem is the same one that faced George Lucas and Steven Spielberg, who weren't happy that critics trashed *Indiana Jones and the Temple of Doom* for being needlessly dark in tone and character, an assessment with which George Lucas and Steven Spielberg reluctantly agreed some years later. Disney will have to turn this ship around by making a third film that is more story and less needless action. I'm sure all hands on deck have seen the *Dead Man's Chest* reviews—positive and negative—and are eager to go back to the drawing board to put the emphasis back on the storytelling and minimize the eye candy. Mind you, I liked the second film, but I would have preferred to say I loved it, as I did the first film—a sentiment I share with my nephew.

Let's hope Disney goes to the ends of the Earth to get the third film in ship-shape and whet our appetites for *Pirates* #4.

The DVDs

Curse of the Black Pearl

On disc #1, skip immediately to chapter seven to bypass the usual previews and go directly to the menu. You can watch the movie itself or enjoy it with audio commentaries by Gore Verbinski (director), Johnny Depp (Jack Sparrow), Jerry Bruckheimer (producer), Keira Knightley (Elizabeth Swann), Jack Davenport (Commodore Norrington), and its screenwriters, Ted Elliot and Terry Rossio.

If you have a computer, more features are available including the script and movie side-by-side and a storyboard viewer that shows shot-by-shot conceptual drawings with their corresponding movie shots.

Disc #2 is jam-packed with all sorts of visual goodies:

"An Epic at Sea"—The making of *Curse of the Black Pearl*, an in-depth documentary of how the film was made

"Diary of a Ship," which follows the *Interceptor* (the *Lady Washington* in real life) from its home port of Seattle, Washington, to its final destination, the Caribbean islands

"Diary of a Pirate," which takes you behind the scenes to see a day in the life of a pirate through the eyes of actor Lee Arenberg, the pirate Pintel in the film

Producer's Photo Diary with Jerry Bruckheimer, which is how the filming looked from his unique perspective

"Fly on the Set," featurettes which show how select scenes were shot

A blooper reel

"Below Deck," an interactive history of pirates

Deleted and alternate scenes

"Moonlight Serenade" Scene Progression, a transformational view of Barbossa's pirates turning from human to the living dead—from storyboards to the final film

From the Disney television vault, a portion of "Disneyland from Pirates of the Caribbean to the World of Tomorrow," with Walt Disney himself previewing the ride prior to its official launch

Image galleries, with sideshows of various storyboards, conceptual art, inspiration, publicity, and promotion

The "Lost" Disc #3

Sold as a package with the two-disk set, this is actually a disc of bonus materials with sixty-nine minutes of featurettes:

"Becoming Captain Jack," Johnny Depp interviewed

"Becoming Barbossa," Geoffrey Rush interviewed

"Thar She Blows!" blowing up the *Interceptor*

"The Monkey's Name Is Jack," a close-up look at the two monkeys that are used in the film

More "Fly on the Set" featurettes, more key sequences from the film

"Pirates around the World," a comparison of the dubbed film versions worldwide

"Spirit of the Ride," the film's principals reflecting on their early memories of the theme park ride

"Dead Men Tell No Tales: The History of the Attraction," a documentary

"Sneak Attack Animatic," animation used to plan this key movie scene

Dead Man's Chest

Dead Man's Chest is available as a one-disc or a two-disc special edition. The one-disc version features the film itself, audio commentary by screenwriters Ted Elliott and Terry Rossio, and bloopers.

Disc #2 is a bonus disc with over five hours of special features:

"Captain Jack: From Head to Toe," secrets and legends revealed by Johnny Depp and others

"Dead Men Tell New Tales: Re-Imagineering the Attraction"

"Pirates on Main Street: The World Premiere"

"Meet Davy Jones: Discover the Creation, Mystery, and Mythology of the Sea's Ghostly Ruler"

"According to Plan," a journal of filming the movie

"Charting the Return," a preproduction diary

"Fly on the Set," featurette on the bone cage

"Creating the kraken"

"Mastering the Blade," sword-fighting with the film's stars

"A Producer's Photo Diary" with Jerry Bruckheimer

Multiplayer Online Game

For those who want to enjoy the swashbuckling life without any of the hardships, why not try the multiplayer online game? "In the game, players will interact with Jack Sparrow, Will Turner, Elizabeth

Swann, and other popular characters from the movie franchise, as they embark on exciting quests in search of treasure and notoriety," according to its official website, pirateslegend.com.

Players embark on quests for adventure and treasure in an effort to become the Caribbean's most legendary pirate. Featuring hundreds of customization options, players create and customize their own pirate, form a crew, and set sail on the high seas. Along the way they will interact with and learn skills from the notorious Jack Sparrow, forge alliances with thousands of other players, hunt for buried treasure on uncharted isles, battle evil undead forces, and face off against numerous enemies on land and sea.

Video games

For fans who want a virtual "hands on" experience, three Pirates of the Caribbean games are currently available on multiple platforms. "Pirates of the Caribbean" is very loosely based on the ride and movie; the only resemblance is that you are a pirate in the Caribbean. "Pirates of the Caribbean: The Legend of Jack Sparrow" features the voice of Johnny Depp as Captain Jack and recounts some of his past adventures. "Pirates of the Caribbean: Dead Man's Chest" is based on the second movie and also features the voice of Johnny Depp. For more information, check out detailed reviews on gamespot.com.

Pirate Booty

Disney is known for its marketing genius by producing a full line of "must have" collectibles and memorabilia. Of the hundreds of items available, here's my short list of what I'd want to add to my treasure chest.

1. The film soundtracks ($19 each)

2. The 18 inch Jack Sparrow statue; hand-painted, and limited to only 1,000 pieces ($180)

3. Any of the action figures (4 inches) manufactured by Zizzle: Jack Sparrow, Davy Jones, Will Turner, Elizabeth Swann, "Bootstrap" Bill, Pintel, Palifico, and others ($6 each)

4. A color poster with pirate art, used for the theme park ride at New Orleans Square in Disneyland; the poster measures 36 x 53 inches ($120)

5. A cursed Aztec coin necklace plated in 24K gold from the Noble Collection ($129)

6. A set of three ships (the *Flying Dutchman*, the *Black Pearl*, and *Edinburgh Trader*) from Zizzle ($70)

7. Any of the movie posters ($10–20)

8. A pair of pirate ship bookends (the *Flying Dutchman* and the *Black Pearl*) from disneyshopping.com ($99.95)

9. Jack Sparrow Big Figure, 22-inch-high resin statue from Disney ($150)

10. Pirates of the Caribbean picture frame (for 4 x 6 photo)

Disneyland Resort: *Where to Stay*

It is perhaps the best-kept secret in Disneyland: a pirate hideaway for the *Pirates of the Caribbean* movie fan who wants lodgings to match his piratical mood. Atop the Sierra Tower at the Disney Hotel, located at the Disneyland Resort, there's a "Pirates of the Caribbean Suite." Formerly one of the hotel's Presidential Suites, the room has been completely remodeled. It's a one-of-a-kind room, not available at any other Disney hotel property in the world. Here's what to expect:

An assigned vacation planner to help you with your Disneyland Resort stay

A special toy for kids

A doorbell that plays, "Yo Ho, Yo Ho, a Pirate's Life for Me"

Overhead wooden beams and a dark-stained floor covered with Old World rugs

Spanish colonial style furnishings in keeping with the seventeenth century

Modern conveniences: a wet bar, a 42-inch plasma television, and a surround sound stereo system

A master bedroom, known as the "Captain's Quarters," that has a four-poster bed, cast-iron lighting fixtures, and artwork on the walls inspired by *Pirates of the Caribbean*

A second nautically inspired bedroom for kids

Locked display cases with a replica of Jack Sparrow's revolver, pirate figurines, a replica of the "Dead Man's Chest," and more

Better plan on finding a treasure chest to pay for the room, though. Call 714-956-MICKEY for more information.

Walt Disney World Resort: *Where to Stay*

There's something for everyone at the world's most popular resort complex, but pirate fans will want to stay at Caribbean

Beach in the Epcot area. According to Birnbaum's *Walt Disney World: The Official Guide*:

> Guests check in at the Custom House, a reception building that projects the feeling of a tropical resort. Décor, furnishings, and staff costumes all reflect the Caribbean theme. Old Port Royale, a complex near the center of the property, evokes images of an island market. Stone walls, pirates' cannons, and tropical birds and flowers add to the atmosphere.

Its telephone number is 407-934-3400. The room, which is designed for four guests, has a variable rate depending on the time of year; check online at disney.com for the current prices.

The Disney Gallery, which hosted the *Pirates of the Caribbean* movie exhibit at New Orleans Square, Disneyland Park, Anaheim, California.

MOVIE EXTRAS WANTED

PIRATES:

Extreme characters and hideously unattractive types, ages 18-50. Odd body shapes or very lean to extremely skinny. Missing teeth, wandering eyes, and serial killer looks with real long hair and beards. Wigs and make-up are not what we are looking for. We also need little people, very large sumo wrestler types, extremely tall or extremely short people, albinos, amputees. Any size or shape that is **NOT** average is best.

—*Casting call for pirate-types for* Pirates of the Caribbean *movie number three*

PIRATE CASTING CALL

As any native knows, life in Los Angeles has its disadvantages—the traffic, the unreal cost of real estate, high taxes, etc. But for anyone with film aspirations, Los Angeles is The Place to Be. In December 2004, Sande Alessi Casting company in Los Angeles was tasked with finding extras for the third *Pirates of the Caribbean* movie. As one online story explained, it drew more than seven thousand aspirants: A few were in full pirate costume, while others suggested how they might look with accessories including hats, vests, frock coats, boots, swords, prop pistols, beaded hair dangles, do-rags, tattoos, belts, and various types of bling including rings, necklaces, headbands, and bracelets, usually in multiples. Not surprisingly, they weren't looking for picture-perfect people; they were looking for a distinct type, characterized by a lean and hungry look—the look of pirates!

According to Alessi, ideal pirate crew extras should be scrawny (real pirates tended to live on vegetables and rum), with long hair and beards. She was especially looking for people with a really emaciated look, some pirate reenactor experience, sailing or tall ship experience (including the ability to climb masts, rig sails, and row), amputees, and people with removable body parts such as eyes and teeth.

They were also looking for female extras to play the part of various citizenry.

Although casting for *Pirates of the Caribbean: At World's End* is complete, casting calls will be needed in the future because of future films in the series, so there may yet be an opportunity to find yourself in one of the future films if you can look and act the part.

Check out sandealessicasting.com for updates.

A miniature model handcrafted by August F. Crabtree,
on exhibit at the Mariners' Museum, Newport News, Virginia.

8. WHAT'S YOUR PIRATE I.Q.?

"Swashbuckler: The Romance of the Pirate"
display at the Mariners' Museum.

We've covered a lot of ground about the golden age of pirates, but if you want real pirate "cred," you need to know where you stand. Try this true-or-false quiz to find out. The answer key immediately follows the questions. I've provided detailed answers, rather than simply stating true or false. Trust me, by the time you finish this quiz, you'll know a lot more about nautical terms, pirate lore, historical information, and geographical information. Although we've already covered many of these topics, some are new and might require a little homework on your part.

True or False:

1. The golden age of piracy was in the sixteenth century.

2. Pirates raided ships of any nationality.

3. Davy Jones' locker is the traditional name given to the ship captain's personal locker located in his quarters.

On the bow of the ship, the planked area served as the bathroom facilities. On the replicated ship, *Godspeed,* at the Jamestown Settlement.

4. A poop deck is where pirates went to the bathroom at sea.

5. A rapier was the preferred sword for ship-to-ship fighting.

6. A Spanish doubloon was a silver coin.

7. A Spanish galleon is a liquid unit of measure used to ration rum.

8. When someone let the "cat out of the bag" it meant that they took the ship's feline below deck to hunt the rats that infested the ship.

9. Pirates always made their victims walk the plank.

10. Holystone was a good luck talisman favored by sailors.

11. "Jolly Roger" was the nickname of Jack Roger. It referred to his jovial nature.

12. A compass can be used to measure longitude and latitude.

13. A league is a nautical term of measure that equals five miles at sea.

14. List is a nautical term meaning a handwritten compilation of goods stored below deck.

15. The pirate expression, "no quarter given," means that when pirates were on land and needed change from a barmaid,

they preferred her to keep the change as a tip; therefore, she need not give back change in quarters.

16. Port is a nautical term meaning the ship's hold is carrying a significant amount of wine.

17. Starboard is a nautical term referring to the left side of the ship, facing forward.

18. To "dance the hempen jig" was a favorite pirate dance, usually performed when a pirate was stone drunk, and usually at taverns during shore leave.

19. The pirate popularly known as Blackbeard holds the record for the greatest number of ships captured.

20. According to historical records, the vessel most often used by pirates was a schooner.

21. Blackbeard's ship was called *Queen Anne's Revenge.*

22. A peg leg (wooden leg) is merely pirate myth.

23. Pirates practiced autocracy on board the ship. The ship's captain had final say all the time.

24. A favorite snack among pirates, known for its delicious taste, was a dessert ironically called hardtack.

25. Pirates usually lived to a ripe old age.

26. Some pirates wore eye patches because they had to stare at the sun when using a navigational instrument called a cross-staff.

A backstaff on display at the Mariners' Museum.

27. Vaporing is a specific pirate term meaning raising a big stink before boarding a ship by screaming loudly and making a lot of noise with their weapons, in an attempt to scare the living daylights out of their intended prey.

28. The pirate flags of Christopher Moody and Henry Every were red in color, whereas most pirate flags are black in color.

29. A flintlock pistol was the preferred weapon when boarding an enemy vessel because it was accurate at long ranges and could be reloaded quickly.

30. When a pirate made you "governor of an island," it meant that you had, in effect, received a death sentence: You were marooned on a remote island.

31. Pirates were routinely branded on their forearms. This way it was easy to see whether or not a suspicious person was a law-abiding citizen or a scurvy sea dog who deserved to be hung.

32. Lieutenant Maynard of the Royal Navy is best remembered for cutting off the head of Blackbeard and hanging it from his sloop.

33. Anne Bonny and Mary Read were female pirates who served under "Calico Jack" Rackham.

34. When boarding an enemy ship, the first pirate across—if he survived—got first choice of any seized weapons because of his risk.

35. Pirates were usually barefoot on deck.

36. A pistol had a heavy brass butt, so it could be used as a club during close-in, hand-to-hand combat.

37. A gun (often mistakenly called a cannon) onboard a ship was a formidable weapon because it could traverse, elevate, and fire with pinpoint accuracy.

38. The captain's quarters aboard a large ship were usually positioned at the front of the ship so he could get the best possible view of what lay ahead.

39. A powder monkey was a capuchin monkey trained to hand small bags of powder to the gunner manning the shipboard guns.

40. A broadside refers to a fat pirate.

41. Keelhauling was a particularly nasty, often fatal, method of punishment that involved tossing a man overboard and pulling him under the bow of the ship.

42. A carpenter was a highly prized member of the crew.

43. Each pirate ship drafted its own articles, which were the rules they lived by.

A carpentry tool used by a shipbuilder, on display at the Mariners' Museum.

44. The most famous novel about pirates is *Treasure Island* by Robert Louis Stevenson.

45. Pirates enjoyed gambling; cards and dice were two of their vices.

46. Cackle fruit was slang for chicken eggs.

A slot adze, "used to cut and dress wood surfaces, such as the top of a keel or the face of a frame." On display at the Mariners' Museum.

47. The famous Disney ride, Pirates of the Caribbean, was considered a premiere ride. It was called an "E" ticket ride.

48. Captain Jack Sparrow commands a ship called the *Flying Dutchman*.

49. Careening a ship meant deliberately beaching it so that maintenance—removing seaweed and barnacles—could be done to improve its seaworthiness and enhance its speed.

50. Tortuga, a Caribbean island, was a favored pirate haven.

51. Seen in the movie *Curse of the Black Pearl*, Port Royal in Jamaica is an actual Caribbean seaport.

52. The mostly common booty found on a ship raid was the coveted treasure chest, usually filled with gold and silver coins, pearls, and priceless gems.

53. Pirates didn't buy their ships; they simply stole them.

54. Captain Jack Sparrow's tricorne hat is made of leather. A traditional tricorne hat is made of felt.

A treasure chest on display at the Mariners' Museum.

55. A woman was considered good luck aboard a pirate vessel.

56. A medicine chest was considered an especially valuable prize when looting another ship.

57. If a man said he was currently employed in "the sweet trade," it meant that he was a pirate by profession.

58. Sea turtles were a favorite delicacy on a ship.

59. The lookout post on the main mast was called the crow's nest.

60. In the sixteenth century, round shot (iron balls) fired from a ship's gun had an explosive mixture inside.

A medicine chest on display at the Mariners' Museum.

61. A backstaff allowed a navigator to stand with his back to the sun to take measurements of latitude.

62. Spanish maps and map books were so highly prized among pirates that at least one Spanish captain threw them overboard, rather than let them fall into enemy hands.

A replica of a map used in the movie *Goonies,* with "X" marking the spot. On display at the Mariners' Museum.

63. Due to frequent clubbings on their heads during ship raids, pirates suffered from bad memory; consequently, it was necessary to place a large X on maps, so they wouldn't forget where they buried their booty.

64. A pirate captain sometimes dressed as a gentleman, especially when going ashore, wearing fine clothes usually obtained by theft after raiding a merchant ship.

65. Records show that approximately 1,500 to 2,000 pirates roamed the Caribbean and northern waters, and the average pirate crew was eighty men.

66. Some of Blackbeard's men were tried, sentenced to be hung, and then hung in Williamsburg, Virginia.

67. "Black Bart" Bartholomew Roberts was the most successful pirate in his day, capturing an estimated 400 ships.

68. Most sunken treasure can be found off the coast of Florida.

69. Pirates sometimes disguised their intentions by raising the flags of friendly nations, by disguising the cargo on the deck to make it appear to be a civilian craft, by covering their gunports, and by dressing up as women—all to lull their prey into a false sense of security.

70. The second in command on a pirate ship was the quartermaster.

71. A normal merchant ship, which had a few dozen men at best and up to six guns, usually surrendered to pirates without a fight.

72. A little-known fact brought to light in *Curse of the Black Pearl*, Aztec gold is always cursed, traced back to Cortes' looting of that ancient empire.

73. When pirates did have money, they usually gambled or threw the money away during shore leave.

74. The average pirate was single and in his twenties.

75. Gibbet refers to a specific kind of brown gravy that pirates liked to dip biscuits in to improve their flavor.

76. A flintlock musket was a sharpshooter's weapon, used to pick off a ship's captain or other high-ranking personnel in an attempt to demoralize the enemy.

77. The greatest cause of death for pirates was disease.

78. On an extended cruise, when pirates ran low on food, they resorted to boiling leather for consumption.

79. Water was the most frequently consumed beverage aboard a pirate ship.

80. A landlubber is a person who has no knowledge of nautical matters, no skills at seamanship, and generally is slow to get his sea legs.

81. There were provisions to compensate pirates for injuries obtained in battle. Generally speaking, the limbs that

warranted the most compensation (hundreds of pieces of eight) were either the right leg or right arm.

82. Flogging the monkey meant rinsing out a small cask of rum with water to get what little alcohol was left inside.

83. The pirate's motto was "No prey, no pay."

84. A punch house was a place where a pirate could get a wide selection of tropical juices.

85. *Queen Anne's Revenge* was the name Blackbeard gave to a ship formerly known as the *Concord* under British command and the *Concorde* under French command.

86. A "snotty" was a midshipman, a young boy, who had aspirations of becoming an officer on a ship. The expression refers to the practice of him using his jacket sleeves to wipe the snot from his nose.

87. A ship surgeon was in fact trained as a doctor.

88. A dead man's chest was pirate slang for a coffin.

89. Pirates traded in anything of value, including African slaves.

90. Pirates used a spyglass to spot distant ships.

A pirate uses a spyglass to look at ships in the harbor.
(Photo courtesy of Pirates in Paradise Festival in Key West, Florida.)

Scoring:

80 answers correct or more, the grade of A

75 – 79 answers correct, the grade of B

60 – 74 answers correct, the grade of C

55 – 59 answers correct, the grade of D

Below 55, a failing grade

SHIP POSTINGS:

A
Avast! You've just been promoted to
captaincy of your own ship!

B
A worthy effort indeed, sir! You can take the post
of quartermaster on the ship of your choice. Yo ho!

C
Welcome aboard!
You're the new first mate.

D
It's the crow's nest for you!

F
Squawk! Walk the plank!

Answer Key:

1. FALSE.

No two experts can agree on the exact dates of the golden age of pirates, but most agree it was a short-lived period. Pirate expert Pat Croce puts it at 1690–1730, a mere forty years. David Cordingly, author of *Under the Black Flag*, says it began in 1690 and came to "an abrupt end around 1725, when naval patrols drove the pirates from their lairs and mass hangings eliminated many of their leaders. It is this period which has inspired most of the books, plays, and films about piracy, and has been largely responsible for the popular image of the pirate in the West today."

2. TRUE.

The general public uses the words pirate, buccaneer, and privateer interchangeably, which has lent to the confusion. To clarify: A **pirate** is a person who preyed on ships of any nationality, a **buccaneer** (from the French word Boucanier) preyed on the French and Spanish, and a **privateer** is a person who had legal authority from a specific country to raid ships of any opposing nationality. It's worth noting that the ranks of pirates swelled because some were former privateers who turned to the only trade they knew, some were press-ganged (that is, forced to join), some were former slaves, and others joined voluntarily.

3. FALSE.

The ship's captain likely had a sea chest in which to store personal goods, but Davy Jones' locker refers to a watery grave, the bottom of the ocean. Davy Jones was considered by mariners to be a sea devil, but not in the literal sense as interpreted by Disney in the *Pirates of the Caribbean* films. No doubt new generations of fans will confuse the Disney version with the actual myth.

4. FALSE.

The poop deck is located aft (that is, the rear) on a ship. Below it is the poop cabin. The term has nothing to do whatsoever with bathroom functions. In those days, on a large ship like the *Black Pearl,* pirates relieved themselves on wooden seats (comfort seats) cut with an open bottom, so the waste simply fell into the ocean. Larger ships had small seats below deck with pipes carrying refuse out, but this primitive setup, which should not be confused with modern plumbing, would likely have been used at night or during times of bad weather when it would have been dangerous or uncomfortable to use the deck-side comfort seats. On modern ships, the bathroom facility is called the head. No sailor would say, "I'm going to the bathroom." A sailor would say, "I'm going to the head."

5. FALSE.

A rapier is long, and its design is not practical for close-in, one-on-one fighting on a ship's deck with rigging everywhere. A short sword is ideal because it does not get caught up in the rigging. Hence the cutlass is perfect: short but heavy and razor sharp.

6. FALSE.

A doubloon was a Spanish gold coin; silver coins came in several denominations (2 reale, 4 reale, and 8 reale).

7. FALSE.

A Spanish galleon was a ship, not a measurement of rum. Rum was usually allocated daily with a brass cup called a rum measurer in the amount of one-half Gill (two shots by today's standards).

8. FALSE.

Letting the cat out of the bag is a contemporary expression that means a secret was announced prematurely. In the seventeenth century, the cat was a cat-o'-nine-tails, so when it was taken out of its bag for use it meant that someone was in for a flogging.

9. FALSE.

Walking the plank is pure fiction, reinforced by popular literature (*Peter Pan* and *Treasure Island*) and popular movies. In cases when victims weren't spared, they were simply killed and tossed overboard.

10. FALSE.

Holystone was used to scrub the deck of the ship. According to one source, it was also called the "holy" stone because sailors were in a kneeling, penitent position when scrubbing the deck.

11. FALSE.

The words "Jolly Roger" came from the French. It's not a reference to a specific pirate but to the flags that were raised by pirates to announce their true colors.

12. FALSE.

A compass is used to measure direction only. To determine latitude, navigators used an instrument called a cross-staff; it was subsequently replaced by the backstaff. (Replicas of these period instruments are available at http://home.comcast.net/~saville/back staffhome.html.) Measuring longitude, however, was a different matter: It wasn't effectively measured until 1736, when John Harrison developed the marine timekeeper. This was not merely a problem to solve. A considerable computational error could be disastrous, often meaning life or death. (For more information, go to www.history.com/encyclopedia.do?articleId=217414.)

13. FALSE.

A league is a form of measurement. One league is three statute miles or approximately 4,828 meters.

14. FALSE.

List means a ship's tilt to one side. If a ship lists too far—as when guns on the ship have all rolled to one side—the ship cannot right itself and will capsize.

15. FALSE.

No quarter given means that when a pirate is engaging in combat, no mercy will be given. It's a fight to the finish. It's understood that pirates didn't expect any quarter, either, under the circumstances.

16. FALSE.

Port means the left side of the ship as you look forward.

17. FALSE.

Starboard means the right side of the ship as you look forward.

Detail on a miniature ship hand-carved by August F. Crabtree, on exhibit at the Mariners' Museum.

18. FALSE.

To "dance the hempen jig" meant hanging, usually at the end of a hemp rope. When hung, the victim's feet would "dance"—that is to say, jerk involuntarily.

19. FALSE.

Blackbeard is the most famous pirate, but the record was held by Black Bart, whose real name was Bartholomew Roberts; he captured 400 ships.

20. TRUE.

The schooner was in fact the most commonly used ship, according to David Cordingly, author of *Under the Black Flag*.

21. TRUE.

The *Concorde* was a French ship, captured from the English. When Blackbeard captured it from the French, he renamed it *Queen Anne's Revenge*.

22. FALSE.

A peg leg is a prosthesis, an artificial limb. A wooden leg was not unusual, since shipboard accidents were common. Even when not in combat, pirates could suffer injuries such as a crushed or severed leg. As any contemporary sailor would tell you, being on the deck of a ship is simply dangerous. This is why commercial fishing is considered a dangerous profession—one of the most hazardous, in fact.

23. FALSE.

Though pirates were outlaws, they still had to have rules to live by. The ship's articles, which varied from ship to ship, specified those rules. Autocracy was practiced by the military, but pirates practiced democracy. Other than when engaged in combat, the crew could vote their ship's captain out of power.

24. FALSE.

Sometimes called a sea biscuit, hardtack was filling but hardly a treat (like, say, a donut). Hardtack had as its virtue the ability to stay "fresh" for prolonged periods of time, whereas other foodstuffs might spoil. It was not a favorite, of course, but better than no food at all.

25. FALSE.

Pirates led a hard, fast life, and if disease didn't get them, they usually found themselves at the end of ropes.

26. TRUE.

A cross-staff was used to determine latitude, but it meant staring directly into the sun. Prolonged staring, of course, caused permanent eye damage, which is why a pirate might wear an eye patch. Of course, he could also sustain an eye injury during hand-to-hand combat or a shipboard injury during periods of noncombat.

The invention of the backstaff, which allowed measurements to determine latitude by putting one's back to the sun, made the cross-staff obsolete.

27. TRUE.

Pirates preferred to intimidate their victims into surrendering, which saved lives on both sides. The preferred method was to make as big a commotion as possible, called vaporing, to frighten the enemy into submission. It almost always worked, I would think.

28. TRUE.

Most pirate flags were black, but a red flag was even more feared because it meant that no quarter would be given.

29. FALSE.

If available, a flintlock pistol was indeed a favorite weapon to carry when boarding an enemy ship. At close range it was deadly and could kill someone before coming into sword-fighting range, but it could not be reloaded quickly, which is why a pirate was customarily armed with a cutlass and a dagger. If a pirate had more than one pistol, he usually expended all before resorting to his cutlass. Blackbeard was known to carry up to four pistols, each secured to him, to inflict maximum damage. Even when expended, however, a pistol was still useful.

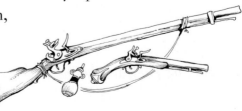

The heavy butt, usually made of copper, was a deadly weapon in its own right.

30. TRUE.

"Governor of an island" was a mocking phrase. The victim indeed governed over an island, but he was the *only* one on the island. In time, due to starvation or the use of the single shot, the population decreased by exactly one soul.

31. FALSE.

Pirates were not branded on the forearm. According to the writers who researched pirates for *Pirates of the Caribbean*, the East India Trading Company branded pirates on the forehead. I haven't been able to confirm this independently, so I'll have to take their word for it until I can verify otherwise.

32. TRUE.

Blackbeard, unlike some of his shipmates, never had a trial. Lieutenant Maynard cut off his head and hung it high from a masthead for all to see. This effectively ended the ship-to-ship battle and also put an end to Blackbeard's bloody reign. Many of Blackbeard's men were killed in battle; afterward, fourteen others were hung in Williamsburg, Virginia, in 1719.

33. TRUE.

Anne Bonny and Mary Read were female pirates who were later tried and sentenced for hanging but escaped that fate by "pleading our bellies," as they put it, meaning, they were pregnant and, by law, couldn't be hung because killing an unborn child was a crime. They were by no means the only female pirates, but they were the most infamous, partly because of the notoriety of their ship's captain, "Calico" Jack Rackham.

34. TRUE.

The most dangerous part of seizing another ship was boarding it. And the most dangerous aspect of boarding it was being the first on board, because it was highly likely that you would be fatally shot or stabbed. Because of the considerable risk involved, the pirate who volunteered to go first was rewarded if he lived (a big *if*). He had the first choice of weapons seized, and he most likely took a pistol, which was highly prized because of its portability and lethality at close range.

35. TRUE.

Pirates were usually barefoot on ship, which can be seen in some turn-of-the-century illustrations. Although going barefoot undoubtedly contributed to a surer footing, I would think the protection afforded by leather shoes would be a consideration against shipboard hazards.

36. TRUE.

Those who designed the flintlock pistol were well aware that reloading was a slow process, so the reinforced butt was designed to make the pistol useful even when it was not loaded. While a quick blow to the head could prove deadly, it would be more likely to knock out your opponent.

37. FALSE.

In the seventeenth century, guns onboard ships were deadly at close range, but problematic at medium and long ranges, hence the expression "a long shot." Though there was a primitive aiming device for elevation only, the fixed guns could not traverse—i.e., move laterally. And because of variations in powder, in the round ball, and in the ramming technique, no two shots hit the same target in the same place. Also, because the guns recoiled three to four feet, thick ropes secured them from rolling back. Because of premature tube wear, a gun was only good for a few hundred shots and then it had to be replaced.

38. FALSE.

The captain's quarters were in the aft part of the ship, in the cabin below the poop deck. The crew's quarters were usually beneath the deck and forward. Sometimes, it'd be a room but often was just space where hammocks were hung for sleeping. Most often, it meant finding any convenient place to catch a few winks.

39. FALSE.

Capuchin monkeys not only made good pets for the crew but also were valuable pets for resale in Europe, where these exotic creatures fetched a good price. In the Royal Navy, a powder monkey transported powder from the onboard storage facility, the ship's magazine, to the gunners.

40. FALSE.

A broadside was a deadly one-volley blast from the ship's onboard guns. Fired at point-blank range, a broadside could significantly damage a ship if enough guns were fired.

41. TRUE.

For minor offenses, the cat-o'-nine-tails was used, but for major offenses, keelhauling, a particularly harsh and often fatal punishment, was employed.

An auger bit ("Wooden shipbuilding requires thousands of holes drilled by an auger to receive the wood or metal pins that hold members together.") and a plated brace ("Originally the auger was a complete tool with its own handle. By the seventeenth century, the brace had been developed with interchangeable bits used for drilling holes of various sizes.") on display at the Mariners' Museum.

42. TRUE.

A ship's carpenter was a valuable member of the crew, no matter his origin. Because the ships were made of wood, ongoing maintenance and repairs were essential to keeping them shipshape.

43. TRUE.

Pirates lived, and sometimes died, by the pirate's code; the specifics of articles varied depending on the ship captain. Crewmembers had to sign the ship's articles, including those press-ganged, though sometimes tradesmen were not required to sign. (By not signing, some tradesmen were able to escape hanging during pirate trials; they rightly claimed to be victims, working in involuntary servitude.)

44. TRUE.

Over the years, *Treasure Island* has been a treasure chest for scores of musicians, writers, artists, and others wanting to capitalize on its storyline. Much of what we celebrate in popular culture about pirates is associated with this formative novel: squawking parrots, buried treasure, maps with "X" marking the spot, peg legs, blind pirates, Long John Silver, the Black Spot, sea chests, etc. Required reading for anyone remotely interested in pirate fiction, *Treasure Island* is the book that launched a thousand pirate ships.

45. TRUE.

When pirates had free time aboard a ship or in port they gambled. Cards and dice were their principal vices. Add liquor and the list is nearly complete. As any sailor knows, monotony on board—in between ship maintenance and combat—is a deadly enemy because the "devil always finds work for idle hands."

46. TRUE.

Fresh food of any kind was always a welcome break from the usual monotonous diet of a pirate. A fresh chicken egg ("cackle fruit") was always welcomed.

47. TRUE.

In the early days of Disneyland, the admission price was separate from the price for individual rides. The coupons, designated A through E, varied in cost, from ten cents for an "A" coupon (a horse car ride on Main Street) to eighty-five cents for an "E" coupon (Pirates of the Caribbean). Later rescinded in favor of a one-price admission policy to the theme parks, the "E" coupon has come to designate a premiere ride, which is why NASA astronaut Sally Ride, the first woman in space, termed the flight of the space shuttle as an "E-ticket ride."

48. FALSE.

Captain Jack Sparrow commands (sporadically, it seems) a ship called the *Black Pearl*. Davy Jones commands the *Flying Dutchman* in *Dead Man's Chest*. According to sea legend, the captain of the *Flying Dutchman,* a ghost ship, is a Dutch sea captain who is doomed to sail the seven seas forever.

49. TRUE.

A pirate ship captain who couldn't pull into port for dry dock maintenance had to beach his ship during low tide to perform necessary, below-the-waterline maintenance. It wasn't an ideal situation by any means, since pirates were especially vulnerable to enemy attack. They were essentially defenseless, since they would not have access to shipboard guns and could not fight off a heavily armed British ship.

50. TRUE.

Tortuga was indeed a favorite pirate haven. According to The Free Encyclopedia at wikipedia.com:

> By 1640, the buccaneers of Tortuga were calling themselves the Brethren of the Coast. The pirate population was mostly made up of French and Englishmen, along with a small number of Dutchmen. . . . By the year 1670, as the buccaneer era was in decline, many of the pirates, seeking a new source of trade, turned to log cutting and trading wood from the island. At this time, however, a Welsh pirate named Henry Morgan started to promote himself and invited the pirates on the island of Tortuga to sail under his flag.

51. TRUE.

Port Royal was indeed a thriving Caribbean town during the golden age of pirates. Protected by several forts in its heyday, the town has lost much of its former luster, though the Jamaican government is trying to revitalize business concerns by developing the area, using its colorful pirate heritage to lure tourists.

52. FALSE.

If there's one myth associated with pirates, it's that a chest of treasure was usually captured in every pirate raiding party. Of course, they were always happy to find such rich plunder, but that wasn't the expectation. Maps, nautical equipment, medical supplies, household goods, clothes, foodstuffs, or barrels of black powder were more commonly found. And what the pirates didn't use for themselves, they needed to replenish the ship's hold. After that, they likely traded or sold whatever was left.

53. TRUE.

Pirates never had the luxury of hiring a shipyard to build a custom boat, so they simply stole (commandeered) ships at sea and traded up, hoping eventually to secure a large boat with gunports.

54. TRUE.

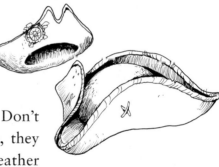

A tricorne hat is traditionally made of felt, though leather would have some advantages: It would wear better (last longer) at sea, could be used to hold water, and could be eaten if softened. Don't laugh; when pirates had no choice, they ate anything edible, including leather goods. (You would, too.)

55. FALSE.

A woman, even a "miniature one" (as Mr. Gibbs refers to young Elizabeth Swann in *Curse of the Black Pearl*), was considered bad luck on a ship. From www.plimsoll.org,

> The traditional view for centuries was that women had no place at sea. They weren't strong enough either physically or emotionally. Men would be distracted and led to vice. Many people thought that having a woman on board would bring bad luck to a ship. A terrible storm was bound to destroy the vessel and everyone on it. This was ancient superstition and deeply ingrained amongst sailors as truth. In later years, the only woman happily accepted on board by many sailors was the figurehead.

56. TRUE.

Medicine was always a prize since it was constantly needed. In fact, Blackbeard once moored off the harbor of Charleston, South Carolina, and held the town hostage until he was given what he wanted: a medicine chest to treat crew members infected by disease—it was nothing to clap about.

57. TRUE.

Pirates didn't call their profession "pirating." They called it "the sweet trade." Sweet, perhaps, because of the freedom; not so sweet, of course, when they faced the hangman.

58. TRUE.

A sea turtle, caught on land, was easy prey for pirates. It was then taken aboard a ship to the bottom of the hold and turned on its back, until it was time to retrieve it for cooking. ("Beautiful soup, so rich and green, waiting in a hot tureen!")

59. TRUE.

According to the *Origin of Navy Terminology*,[2]

> The crow was an essential part of the early sailors' navigation equipment. These landlubbing fowl were carried on board to help the navigator determine where the closest land lay when the weather prevented sighting the shore visually. In cases of poor visibility, a crow was released and the navigator plotted a course that corresponded with the bird's course because it invariably headed straight toward land, "as the crow flies." The crow's cage was situated high in the main mast where the lookout stood his watch. Often, he shared this lofty perch with a crow or two since the crows' cages were kept there: hence the crow's nest.

---

[2]Department of the Navy, Washington, D.C.

60. FALSE.

The round shot was a solid iron ball. It wasn't until the eighteenth century, a full century after the golden age of pirates, that technology developed sufficiently to allow explosive balls made of iron.

61. TRUE.

According to Backstaff Instruments (Marblehead, Massachusetts), a company that sells working replicas for period ships,

The backstaff was a true revolution in navigational instrumentation. All the instruments prior to the invention of the backstaff—the cross-staff, astrolabe, quadrant—required that the user look directly at the sun to take a reading. Not good for the eyes, not to mention lousy for accurate angle measurement. All that changed when John Davis, a sixteenth century English explorer, hit upon the idea of lining up the horizon with the shadow cast by the sun's rays striking a vane. This allowed the user to stand with his or her back to the sun! Marvelous idea! This was an extremely accurate instrument and was used well into the eighteenth century.

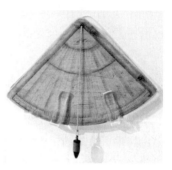

A mariner's quadrant used to determine the altitude of a heavenly body, on display at the Mariners' Museum.

62. TRUE.

Maps were worth their weight in gold. An accurate map was an invaluable navigational tool, especially if it had been drawn from firsthand experience instead of educated guesswork. The Spanish, who traveled from Mexico to Florida and back home, had extremely accurate maps that were prized by pirates. Records show that one Spanish ship captain wept when Spanish maps fell into pirate hands during a raid.

63. FALSE.

No doubt many a pirate got clubbed in the head with the butt of a pistol, but that's beside the point here. For the most part, pirates did not bury treasure, they took it and spent it during shore leave. Therefore, they rarely had maps, much less maps with the treasure locations conveniently marked. Buried treasure is a cherished pirate myth that won't likely go away anytime soon.

64. TRUE.

If you're going to live the part, you have to dress the part. Pirate captains often dressed as gentlemen. Additionally, there are records of pirate ship captains who were hung in all their finery.

65. TRUE.

From David Cordingly's *Under the Black Flag* (p. 202):

Imagine the horrific effect of seeing eighty bloodthirsty pirates "vaporing" and coming close to your ship after the grappling hooks attached to bring the two ships together. Battle-hardened, bloodthirsty, and ready to commit mayhem, who in his right mind would resist?

66. TRUE.

Detailed information on pirate trials and sentencing is available in Daniel Defoe's *A General History of the Pyrates*. According to Colonial Williamsburg's website:

Williamsburg's connection with pirates dates to 1693. Account books of the College of William and Mary show £300 received from three buccaneers named Edward Davis, Lionel Delawafer, and Andrew Hinson, who thus obtained their release from the Jamestown jail. Blackbeard quartermaster

William Howard, while incarcerated in Williamsburg, was defended in court by the town's first mayor, John Holloway, characterized by Spotswood as "a constant patron and advocate of pirates." Nine of Blackbeard's crew survived to be captured and, with six others seized in Bath, were brought to Virginia's colonial capital for trial, probably held in the General Courtroom on the first floor of the Capitol. March 1719 saw thirteen pirates meet their end on the gallows along Williamsburg's present Capitol Landing Road.

67. TRUE.

Though most people are familiar with Blackbeard, it's odd that Black Bart isn't as famous, since he was by far the most successful in terms of capturing ships; ergo, if that's the benchmark by measuring pirate success, Black Bart eclipses Blackbeard.

68. TRUE.

It's worth repeating: There's little evidence to support theories of buried treasure (that is, treasure buried on shore), but there are plenty of wrecks at the bottom of the ocean, which is termed sunken treasure (that is, offshore and underwater) off the Florida coast. Not surprisingly, when a sunken vessel is found, fierce courtroom battles among claimants are inevitable. For instance, when Sub Sea Research found the *Notre Dame de Deliverance* halfway between Florida and Cuba, it claimed salvage rights—rights that were contested by the Spanish government, since it had originally chartered the French vessel. At risk: an estimated $3 billion, according to the BBC, which further noted that "About 250 Spanish ships which sunk in the seventeenth and eighteenth centuries are thought to have taken with them treasure worth [many] billions of dollars."

69. TRUE.

Pirates depended on cover and concealment to allow them to get close enough to an enemy ship without arousing suspicion. When it was too late to flee from the pirate ship, the Jolly Roger was hoisted. Scaring off the prey prematurely meant having to pursue a possibly faster ship, or having to fight nearby warships providing escort protection. The "hit and run, shoot, loot, and scoot" tactics of pirates meant every trick in the book was used to lull the enemy ship into a sense of false security. Then they struck hard and fast!

70. TRUE.

The quartermaster was the senior representative of the ship's crew, who acted as a foreman, overseeing the workload, maintaining discipline, and distributing not only ship supplies but prized booty, as well. After a ship was taken, he would sometimes be put in command of the new ship. In effect, he'd get a field promotion from quartermaster to captain.

71. TRUE.

Merchant ships were no match for pirate ships: Outgunned, outmanned, and inexperienced at combat, the merchant mariners, or seamen, almost always surrendered without a fight, rather than go down to Davy Jones' locker.

72. FALSE.

Cursed gold is pure Hollywood fiction. But it's no fiction that Cortés looted Aztecs of their gold, which had ceremonial (not monetary) value to the Aztec culture and its emperor, Montezuma. The Mexicans may have the last laugh, though, since they are immune to Montezuma's Revenge—a water and food-based bacteria that afflicts gringos in the form of diarrhea.

73. TRUE.

Pirates were spendthrifts, and why not? They lived for today, with their futures hanging in the balance.

74. TRUE.

According to David Cordingly, author of *Under the Black Flag,* pirates were relatively young and unmarried.

75. FALSE.

According to ushistory.org, in Ron Avery's "Philadelphia Oddities: The Gibbet," the gibbet has special significance in pirate history:

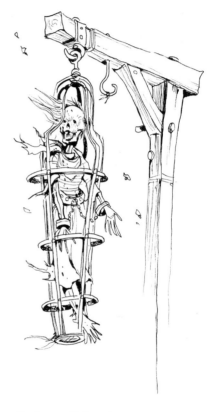

> It's a human form made of iron bands designed to hold the body of an executed criminal for the purpose of public display. The device—more or less—held the rotting corpse together for several weeks. The eighteenth century artifact at the Atwater Kent Museum is America's only complete gibbet. A partial gibbet survives in a museum in Salem, Massachusetts. The primary meaning of the word "gibbet" is simply a gallows. The steel frame to display the culprit's body is properly called a "gibbet iron." But there are references to displaying the body as "gibbeting" and soon the steel frame, itself, was also called "a gibbet."

76. TRUE.

It's a standard military tactic: Decapitate the head and the body will follow. In other words, kill or capture the leadership and the others will fall in line. Of course, firing a flintlock rifle was no easy task on a rolling, pitching ship, providing an unstable platform for shooting a gun with any degree of accuracy.

77. TRUE.

This fact astounds most people, who assume that pirates most often died in combat. To be sure, combat took its toll, but poor hygiene took the biggest toll. A related myth is that pirates, rich from their stolen booty, lived well into their old age, financed by their ill-gotten gains: gold, silver, and precious gems.

78. TRUE.

Desperate times call for desperate measures. Boiled leather is actually palatable and will quell the hunger pangs, but you wouldn't want it as your sole food.

79. FALSE.

Water was stored in barrels in the ship's hold, but it could and did spoil on a long voyage. Therefore, the most common drink was grog, composed in varying parts of rum and water.

The ship's bell on a replica ship moored
at the Jamestown Settlement, Jamestown, Virginia.

80. TRUE.

A civilian can't hope to acquire a sailor's nautical knowledge without years of study and firsthand experience. It takes a long time to know the language, know the ship, and become accustomed to life at sea. When a sailor has his sea legs, he's used to walking on a tossing ship—an acquired skill that obviously can't be duplicated on land.

81. TRUE.

Compensation was usually paid for injuries sustained by pirates during combat. The most compensation was paid for the right arm or leg, then the left arm or leg, and then fingers or eyes.

82. TRUE.

You'd have to be pretty desperate for a taste of rum to flog the monkey, but desperate times call for desperate measures. As Jack Sparrow observed, rum will get you through times with no money better than money will get you through times with no rum.

83. TRUE.

It's called incentive. Necessity is the mother of invention.

84. FALSE.

Pirates didn't drink punch; they drank booze. By the galleon.

85. TRUE.

The name of a ship changed when the ship changed hands. Pirates preferred renaming ships. If you're a pirate short on name inspiration, go to a website called "Pirate Ship Name Generator" at seventhsanctum.com to get a little help.

86. TRUE.

I could elaborate on this at length, but it is not for me to say.

87. FALSE.

A doctor was a trained medical professional—primitive by our standards, but accomplished by the standards of the seventeenth century. A ship's surgeon, however, was not a trained medical professional.

88. TRUE.

The Disney film *Dead Man's Chest* will forever link the phrase with Disney's fictional ship captain, Davy Jones. In fact, a dead man's chest was slang for a coffin.

89. TRUE.

Pirates traded in anything of value, including slaves. The conditions under which African slaves were transported by ship were horrific. The lack of medical attention, inadequate food and water, and poor living conditions took a devastating human toll. According to Robert Falconbridge, author of *An Account of the Slave Trade,* published in 1788, up to 67 percent of the slaves died in transport. A little known fact: Jack Sparrow really does have a moral compass, which became evident when he refused to follow (according to official Disney history) orders to transport African slaves to the New World; instead, he set them free and, by doing so, showed his true colors.

90. TRUE.

A spyglass was an essential piece of equipment. With it, pirates could see distant ships to help determine whether or not to pursue and attack. The spyglass was usually collapsible for easy storage.

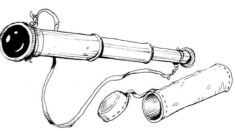

APPENDIX: PORTS OF CALL

Pirate books, pirate movies, pirate websites, and little-known Disney *Pirates of the Caribbean* resources!

1. PIRATE BOOKS

An eight-foot pirate book on display
at the Mariners' Museum. (Note the
sword displayed on an adjacent wall.)

A sea of books about pirates is washing into bookstores nationwide because of the success of the Disney movie franchise *Pirates of the Caribbean*. Now, more than ever, it's become difficult to separate the pyrite from the Spanish doubloons. If you'd rather not wade through dozens of books, the list below names the ones I'd carry in my Sea Bag on a long voyage.

A General History of the Pyrates by Daniel Defoe, edited by Manuel Schonhorn, Dover Publications, 1999. Melding fact and fiction, Defoe's book is one of the few that provide detailed information on what pirates were really like. According to the publisher, "As a commission merchant, importer, ship-owner, and an active journalist who reported 'ship news' and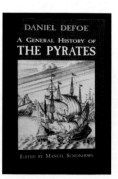

interviewed surviving pirates, Defoe achieved a high degree of authority on the subject of buccaneers. His knowledge was such that [this book] remains the major source of information about piracy in the first quarter of the eighteenth century."

Birnbaum's Walt Disney World 2007,

Disney Editions. If you decide to try the Disney ride that inspired the *Pirates of the Caribbean* movies, you'll need an authoritative guidebook for the Walt Disney World Resort. Get this one. This is the official guidebook for the Orlando resort and is crammed full of insider information, outstanding photography, and delightful Disney art, which the unofficial books cannot hope to match. Also, in the back of the book, you'll find money-saving coupons. Updated annually, this Birnbaum book is especially informative for first-time visitors. There are several related books that are worth your time and money, including Birnbaum's *Walt Disney World for Kids by Kids! 2007,* and Birnbaum's *Walt Disney World Dining Guide 2007.* For those of you who want to explore the Disney theme park in Anaheim, California, I recommend Birnbaum's *Disneyland Resort 2007.*

The Unofficial Guide to Walt Disney World 2007 by Bob Sehlinger with Len Testa,

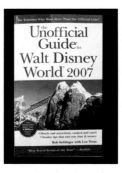

John Wiley & Sons. If you want a different perspective on the Walt Disney World Resort, you may want to check this out. It is, as you'd expect, pretty irreverent and provides a refreshing perspective, with critical comments not beholden to the Big Cheese at corporate Disney.

The Book of Pirates edited and illustrated by Michael Hague, HarperCollins, 2001. An anthology of pirate tales illustrated by renowned children's book illustrator Michael Hague. The wraparound cover is gorgeous: a galleon sailing at night with a skull moon hanging in the sky.

The History of Pirates by Angus Konstam, in association with the Mariners' Museum, with introduction by David Cordingly, The Lyons Press, 2002. If you can only afford one illustrated book about pirates, get this one. Angus Konstam is a former curator of the National Museum of Arms and Armour at the Tower of London; he was also the chief curator at the Mel Fisher Maritime Museum in Key West. In other words, he knows port from starboard. This books gives a historical overview of piracy from the ancient world to contemporary times. Abundantly illustrated with reprinted artwork and photographs, most in full color, this is required reading.

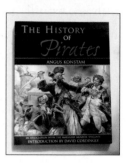

Pirates by John Matthews, Simon & Schuster, 2006. Jumping the gun, this publisher was able to beat *Pirateology* into the bookstore. Similar in size, format, and approach to *Pirateology*, this book is also intended as an overview of pirates for younger readers, though adults will also find the book engaging. Unlike *Pirateology*, this book is a straightforward historical account, not a fictional approach. Young readers will especially enjoy the inserts, which include letters with simulated wax seals, booklets, and foldouts.

Pirateology, Candlewick Press, 2006. Part of an award-winning series including *Egyptology, Dragonology,* and *Wizardology,* this latest addition to a flagship line of illustrated books is intended for younger readers. However, all readers will find this book fascinating because of its unique approach: inserted letters, pullout tabs,  mini-books, and ribboned letters. From the compass inset on the bejeweled cover to a large red jewel on the last page, this book chronicles the adventures of a fictional pirate hunter named Captain William Lubber (surely a deliberate pun) in search of a fictional "vicious and intemperate pirate" named Arabella Drummond. An award winning format with engaging text, illuminating illustrations, and an engaging storyline—this one's pure fun!

Pirate Soul: A Swashbuckling Journey through the Golden Age of Pirates by Pat Croce, Running Press, 2006. Similar in format to *Pirateology* and similar in content to *Pirates,* this book is the best of the bunch. Once you open its Velcro-fastened clasp, the book unfolds  in front of you: The first page is a foldout map of the Caribbean. With reproduced letters, foldout panels, a real feathered quill, inset letters and lists, playing cards, reproduced pages from journals, a gallery of pirates with descriptive histories, and an inside back cover with a simulated compass originally intended to be a working compass, this book is imaginatively designed with authoritative text and lots of photos and illustrations. Pat Croce has an advantage that others attempting books of this nature cannot beat: He owns the largest collection of authentic pirate memorabilia in private hands. The Pirate Soul Museum in Key West is a "must visit" for anyone who wants to see firsthand the artifacts from the golden age of piracy.

Pirates 1660-1730 by Angus Konstam, Osprey, 1998. For anyone desiring a quick overview of the golden age of pirates, this is an excellent informative text with lots of photographs and illustrations, most in full color. Two complaints that I hope will be addressed in future editions—the gutter margin is so tight that  it makes reading the text of the book difficult, and the index is set in type so small that it's unreadable. (Squawk! Walk the plank!)

Pirates: An Illustrated History by Nigel Cawthorne, Chartwell Books, 2006. In addition to this excellent overview of the world of pirates, the author has published several books on military subjects. The book lacks color photographs, essential for any overview book on this colorful subject.

The Pirate Dictionary by Terry Breverton, Pelican Publishing, 2004. The only book of its kind, it thoroughly describes the slang and nautical terms used by pirates and merchant seamen alike from the fifteenth to eighteenth centuries. As is obvious, a lot of common expressions (for example, "rats leaving a sinking ship") had their 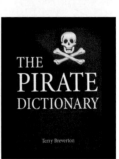 origins hundreds of years ago when the projection of sea power determined a nation's international standing.

Pirates of the Caribbean: Dead Man's Chest adapted by Irene Trimble, based on the screenplay written by Ted Elliott and Terry Rossio, Disney Press, 2006. Intended for younger readers, this is a novelization of the movie. It's fun to read, but its real value is that it preserves the

screenplay in a more reader-friendly format. It includes an eight-page, full-color insert of photos from the film as well.

Pirates of the Caribbean: The Visual Guide by Richard Platt, DK Children, 2007. This oversized (10 x 12.5 inch), full-color book is exactly what it's advertised to be: a visual guide to the first two films. While there is plenty of informative and useful text to add clarity to confusing parts of the movies, the book's real  value can be found in its four-color photographs grouped thematically by subject. For instance, the entry on Davy Jones includes his curiously carved whalebone pipe, the unusually shaped key, and the chest that the key opens. The DK Children book imprint is known for its imaginative approach to book layout that integrates photos with text in a way that invites reading. A visual and textual treat, this book also includes a large pullout folded poster of the *Black Pearl,* giving us the first close-up look at the fastest pirate ship that is, according to Jack Sparrow, "well nigh uncatchable."

Pirates of the Caribbean: From the Magic Kingdom to the Movies by Jason Surrell, Disney Editions, 2006. A superbly written and illustrated book with photos and art covering every aspect of the Disney theme-park ride that inspired the movie, this is an official insider's guide to everything you'd possibly want  to know about one of Disney's most popular rides ever. Of the 144 pages, most are devoted to the theme-park ride; hopefully, future editions will devote more pages to the film franchise.

Pirates! Raiders of the High Seas by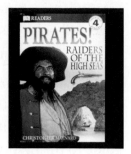
Christopher Maynard, DK Children, 1998.
Intended for young readers, this small but
informative book is designed to give a quick
overview. Like all DK books, this one is imaginatively designed with photographs integrated
into the text to enhance the reading and viewing
experience. A good introduction to the subject for children.

The Pirate Ship: 1660-1730 by Angus
Konstam, Osprey, 2003. Readers who enjoyed
The History of Pirates will no doubt be happy to
learn that Konstam has written more than
twenty books for Osprey Publishing. This short
but informative book is an excellent discussion
of the various vessels used by pirates, from small
sloops to massive warships.

Pirattitude!: So You Wanna Be a Pirate?
Here's How! by John "Ol Chumbucket" Baur
and Mark "Cap'n Slappy" Summers, NAL
Trade, 2005. A fun look at how to get your jol-
lies—your Jolly Rogers, that is! From the guys
who dreamed up "Talk Like a Pirate Day," their
piratical philosophy of "take it easy, have fun,
and show your true colors" permeates this irreverent book. As the
authors make clear, it's all in good fun; they are Sunday pirates and
don't speak the lingo with the fastidiousness of a reenactor, so
don't use this as your only guide if you want to talk like a real
pirate.

See-Through Pirates by Kelly Davis, Running Press, 2003. Intended for kids, this book has "see-through" pages of clear plastic to view before and after scenes. For instance, a see-through page shows a pirate ship during  combat operations, and the page underneath shows the insides of the same ship. A novel way to show history, it's used to good effect in this overview of pirate life.

Spanish Galleon 1530-1690 by Angus Konstam, Osprey, 2004. This book is about the smaller, faster, more maneuverable ship that inspired the English galleon. The Spanish galleon's design is what we most often associate with pirate ships. Excellent full-color photos and illustrations.

Treasure Island by Robert Louis Stevenson, Viking, 1994. If there is one must-read book for pirate fans, that book is surely *Treasure Island*, a classic from which many popular-culture cues about pirates have been derived. The problem is which edition to buy: Of the many dozens of editions, from cheap  reprints in paperback to illustrated hardback editions, what's the edition of choice? There are two, actually. First, the newly reissued Scribner's edition with the N. C. Wyeth illustrations. A facsimile replicating the first edition published in 1911, this $29.99 hard-back hearkens back to the days of yore when artists like Wyeth, Pyle, Parrish, Rockwell, and others dominated the field of book illustration. The other edition worth your money and time is Viking's contextual edition. It starts with the complete text but doesn't end there; the book includes numerous annotations, line drawings, maps, photographs, diagrams, and paintings. For instance, there's a double-page spread on ropework with art, which gives the reader a sense of how important ropework was on a ship. For pure reading enjoyment, stick with Scribner's edition with Wyeth art. But if the reader is also a history buff and wants to know more about the time in which the novel is set, the Viking edition is the clear choice. Either way, you can't go wrong!

Under the Black Flag: The Romance and the Reality of Life among the Pirates by David Cordingly, Random House, 2006. If you know anything about the world of pirates, chances are very good that you've run across one of Cordingly's titles. Interviewed on the bonus disc of *Curse of the Black Pearl,* Cordingly was on  the staff of the National Maritime Museum in Greenwich, England, when he organized several pirate-themed exhibits, including "Captain James Cook, Navigator," "The Mutiny on the Bounty," and "Pirates, Fact and Fiction," which was so popular that it was extended from its four-month slot to three years. If you buy only one book about the history of pirates, buy this one. Cordingly's book, based on the exhibit he organized, is definitive and is often quoted by authors of other books on pirates, including the titles from Osprey Publishing (see listings in this section). Cordingly does a fine job in separating the fiction (the popular-culture interpretations) from the fact, giving us as true a picture as possible of what pirate life was like.

N. C. Wyeth illustration for the endpapers of *Treasure Island.*

GHOST TRAP

by Dave Lowell

Talk about "shiver me timbers!"
Dave Lowell's *Ghost Trap* is a fun read,
a thrilling mixture of ghosts, pirates,
haunted houses, treasure maps, and
spooky things that go bump in the
night. If there ever was a book for a
"dark and stormy night," this is it.

—Horror novelist, Rick Hautala

It's a little-known fact that the infamous Blackbeard was not only the scourge of the Caribbean, but also haunted points further north, all the way up to York, Maine, which is where novelist Dave Lowell lives. No wonder it's where he's chosen to set his first novel, *Ghost Trap*, which uses Blackbeard as a hook to catch the reader's attention.

You'd think that with all the success of pirates on screen, there'd be a lot of pirate novels out there, but there

aren't. In fact, this one—a mildly racy story that's clearly not for children—is one of the few. But it's a corker, as they say in Maine.

Ghost Trap certainly caught my attention when I read it in galley form. According to its author—a lifelong resident of Maine—the inspiration for the novel was Blackbeard himself. Says the author,

> According to legend, Blackbeard visited the Isles of Shoals, just off the coast of Portsmouth, New Hampshire, docking his ship the *Queen Anne's Revenge* and exploring several of the tiny islands. During his brief stay, it is said that he not only married the last of his fourteen brides, but also made her keep secret the location of his hidden treasure.
>
> Spooked by an approaching ship thought to be British military, Blackbeard fled the islands, leaving behind his new bride who never saw him again because he was killed in battle several months later. Legend states that she lived out her days waiting for him to return, never revealing to anyone where he had buried his treasure. Following her death, many locals reported seeing her ghost standing in a long, white cloak before the shoreline, patiently waiting for his ship to return.
>
> In researching the lore of Blackbeard's visit, I found several versions of the tale. Celia Thaxter, a poet who grew up on the islands, claimed in her 1873 book *Among the Isles of Shoals* (University Press of New England, 2003) that Blackbeard did indeed pay a visit. But it was one of his comrades, Captain Scot, who brought along the bride-to-be. Scot made her swear that until his return she would promise to guard over the treasure, hiding it. But most versions state that she married Blackbeard, not Captain Scot. So when writing my novel, I had to decide which tale sounded more accurate and interesting enough to repeat.
>
> Like many storytellers, I also decided to take the liberty of adding my own twist to the age-old tale. I thought to myself: What if Blackbeard not only left behind his last bride, but left her with child? How would his bride be treated by the others on the island? Would they shun her since she was the bride of one of the world's most notorious pirates? And how would mother and child survive among the secluded island colony? Would they become outcasts?

It certainly sounds like perfect reading material for a dark and stormy night when the wind is howling, the rain is pattering against the windowpanes, and tree branches are scratching against the windows. And who knows, maybe there's something else out there, things that go bump in the night? Best to stay inside with the lights on, but they're flickering now, aren't they?

The book is illustrated by Maine artist Glenn Chadbourne, known for his illustrations of Stephen King books. Dave's website is at www.DaveLowell.com, where he's posted a sample chapter, an interview, and photos of York, Maine. Though unsigned copies are available through the usual book sources, buy from Dave and get an inscribed copy. Write to Lowell Collectibles, PO Box 451, York, ME 03909-0451.

Blackbeard and *Ghost Trap* author David Lowell.

"Pirates of the Caribbean: From the Magic Kingdom to the Movies."
A window display at the Disney Marketplace in Anaheim, California.

2. Pirate Movies

DVD technology has allowed many older films, long unavailable on VHS, to be reissued in DVD format. The list that follows includes films specifically designed for children (marked KIDS ONLY) and films for a more general audience, as well.

Blackbeard's Ghost (1968). From Walt Disney, starring Peter Ustinov and Dean Jones. From amazon.com, "In this comedy, Peter Ustinov is the famous pirate's ghost that returns to our time. Blackbeard has been cursed by his last wife who was a notorious witch, so that he will never die. The only way to break the curse is to do—for once in his life—a good act. Is the famous pirate able to do something good?"

Blackbeard: Terror at Sea (2006). A *National Geographic* documentary. From the box copy: "Go inside the cunning mind of a charming criminal genius as *National Geographic* tells the dramatic story of this fearsome pirate who preyed on Caribbean trade routes. Blackbeard charts the exploits of Englishman Edward Teach, an intelligent and charismatic leader who confounded the powers of England and Virginia as he overtook and pillaged forty ships in two years, stealing hidden cargo and precious exports to and from the Caribbean."

The Black Pirate (1926). Starring Douglas Fairbanks. From amazon.com: "A nobleman vows to avenge the death of his father at the hands of pirates. To this end he infiltrates the pirate band. Acting in character he is instrumental in the capture of a ship, but things are complicated when he finds that there is a young woman aboard whom he wishes to protect. . . ."

The Crimson Pirate (1952). Starring Burt Reynolds. From amazon.com: "Notorious raider of the eighteenth century sea lanes, Captain Vallo, known as the Crimson Pirate, and his band of buccaneers overtake a Spanish galleon filled with guns and ammunition. When he decides to sell the stolen arsenal to rebel leader El Libre on the island of Cobra, the representative of Spain, Baron Gruda, offers Vallo 50,000 florins if he will deliver El Libre instead. Vallo is soon caught between the Spanish, the rebellion, and even the mutiny of his own men. But having fallen in love with El Libre's daughter Consuelo, Vallo gains back his crew's trust and leads the island of Cobra to freedom."

Fortunes of Captain Blood and *Captain Pirate* (1950). Two films.

The Goonies (1985). From Warner Home Video, starring Sean Astin and Josh Brolin. KIDS ONLY. Wear earplugs. Lots of screaming kids in this one. From amazon.com, "A group of West Coast kids facing their last days together before a development paves over their homes stumble onto evidence of pirate's treasure, which attracts the attention of a family of criminals."

The Great Ships: The Pirate Ships (1997). A documentary from the History Channel. From amazon.com, "In the golden age of exploration, when Spanish ships loaded with New World gold struggled across the seas to their homeland, one sight feared by all sailors was the Jolly Roger. Under this threatening flag sailed the pirate ships—swift, agile, and dangerous. The great ships take to the high seas alongside the pirates for a thrilling look at one of the most storied chapters in maritime history. Hear tales of legendary pirates like Sir Henry Morgan, whose band of buccaneers captured Panama in 1671! Details of the pirates' life are revealed through their own writings and the stories of those who suffered at their hands. Get an up-close look at the ships that bore the pirates to glory or death through period art and computer reconstructions and see incredible footage of recently discovered pirate and treasure ships in their watery graves. It's a thrilling look at a fabled era and the men and ships whose names have become legend."

Hook (1991). From Sony Pictures, directed by Steven Spielberg, and starring Dustin Hoffman, Robin Williams, Julia Roberts, Bob Hoskins, and Maggie Smith. Despite its all-star cast, the film doesn't enchant. Williams is the boy who did grow up; he's forty years old, and he's forgotten what it's like to be a kid, but a trip back to Neverland takes him back to his magical origins.

Legendary Pirate Movies: Captain Kidd, The Son of Monte Cristo, Long John Silver's Return to Treasure Island (1941). An anthology.

Peter Pan (1953). Timeless animated classic from Disney. Says Doug Thomas from amazon.com, "Unlike some classics, Peter Pan never ages along the way." Enchanting film!

Peter Pan (2003). Starring Jason Isaacs and Jeremy Sumpter. An engaging retelling with a cast of English child-actors who steal the show.

Pirate Kids: Blackbeard's Lost Treasure (2004). KIDS ONLY. "While visiting his grandmother on the coast of North Carolina, a young boy discovers a map and several clues which lead him and his two friends on a quest for buried treasure. But the kids aren't the only ones after the loot."

Pirates of the Caribbean: The Curse of the Black Pearl (2003). From Walt Disney Pictures. Starring Johnny Depp, Geoffrey Rush, Orlando Bloom, and Keira Knightly. This normally comes in a two-disc set, but some were packaged with a bonus third disc promoted as the "lost" disc. Since this is the film that created a resurgence of interest in pirates, it's the first port of call. The first disc contains the movie itself; the second disc contains more than ten hours of supplementary material.

Pirates of the Caribbean: Dead Man's Chest (2006). From Walt Disney Pictures. This is available as a single disc or in a two-disc set. The first disc contains the movie itself; the second disc contains nine featurettes. In a special promotion, not available elsewhere, Best Buy gave away with the purchase of the two-disc set a bonus disc of *Dead Man's Chest* with "exclusive bonus footage" that includes a behind-the-scene features, a photo gallery, and other offerings.

Pirates of the Caribbean: At World's End (2007). From Walt Disney Pictures. To be available as a single- and double-disc set.

The Pirate Movie (1982). Starring Kristy McNichol and Christopher Atkins. A takeoff on the classic, *Pirates of Penzance*. From imdb.com, "Buckle Your Swash and Jolly Your Roger for the Funniest Rock 'N Rollickin' Adventure Ever!"

The Princess and the Pirate (1944). From MGM, starring Bob Hope. From amazon.com: "Princess Margaret is traveling incognito to elope with her true love instead of marrying the man her father has betrothed her to. On the high seas, her ship is attacked by pirates who know her identity and plan to kidnap her and hold her for a king's ransom. Little do the cutthroats know that she will be rescued by that unlikeliest of knights errant, Sylvester the Great, who will lead them on a merry, and madcap, chase."

Real Pirates of the Caribbean (2006). A documentary from Highland Entertainment. From amazon.com, "A history of piracy through the ages. With actual pirate ship footage and real life accounts, this extraordinary documentary captures the true essence of what it means to be a pirate, whether two hundred years ago . . .

or two weeks ago. [This film] will investigate the truth behind the legends of history's most infamous pirates, as well as look at modern day piracy on the open seas."

Treasure of Pirate's Point (1998). KIDS ONLY. From amazon.com, "There's a treasure chest of gold buried on Pirate's Point. When the living descendant of legendary pirate Captain Vane lets Ray in on the secret, there's mutiny in town. Now, Ray and his friends are on a mission to recover the loot and foil an evil plan. In the meantime, they learn that friendship is the most precious treasure of all."

The Ultimate Pirate Collection (2006). Contains various pirate movies, including: *Captain Kidd* (1945), *Corsair* (1931), *Hell Ship Mutiny* (1957), *Jamaica Inn* (1939), *Colossus and the Amazon Queen* (1960), *Law of the Sea* (1931), *League of the Sea Wolf* (1975), *Long John Silver's Return to Treasure Island* (1955), *Mutiny* (1952), *Sea Devils* (1931), *The Black Pirate* (1926), *Windjammer* (1937), *The Mutiny on the Elsinore* (1937), and fourteen installments of "The Adventures of Long John Silver" that ran on television.

Movie posters for *Captain Blood, The Pirates of the Penzance,* and *Swashbuckler,* on display at the Mariners' Museum.

From the outdoor show "Sirens of Treasure Island"
in Las Vegas, Nevada (photo courtesy of Treasure Island).

3. General Pirate Websites

The first place most people go when looking for pirate-related websites is the pirate's web ring at www.ringsurf.com (search using the keyword "pirate"). I've gone through and looked at all the sites to provide this alphabetized listing of the sites that might prove of interest to you. As always, websites—especially fan sites, personal sites, and MySpace sites—come and go, so be forewarned.

Adventures of Dorianne the Pirate (www.katyberry.com).

A fun website with rollovers using a ship's cabin. Music, stories, galleries, ship's tour, pirates, galley, etc. Lots of fun. Check it out. On her homepage, click on the third window on the top row; then click ENTER to explore her piratical world.

Atlantic Buccaneers (www.atlanticbuccaneers.com).

Known as Buccaneers of the Atlantic Coast, this is a group of pirate fans based on the East Coast of the US that "participates in children's events, marches in parades, and performs stage combat routines."

Bilgemunky.com (www.bilgemunky.com).

A general-interest website with news, reviews, and commentary. Its mission statement:

> Growing up a pirate can be difficult, especially in a family of naval tradition—sure, we were all fond enough of ships and oceans, but pillaging was frequently an item of contention. Even so, my parents still found it in their law-abiding hearts to take me to Disney World to ride Pirates of the Caribbean—even bought me a hat. And they willingly took

me to a shrimp festival in Georgia, full in the knowledge that a crew of scurvy pirates roamed freely, kidnapping folks for charity. I wasn't lucky enough to be kidnapped, but I did get to try my first corndog. Heck, my dear folks even took me to Long John Silver's now and then. Pirates were an integral part of my upbringing—just as they may have been a part of yours. Pirates are, after all, a staple of our culture. This has been especially true of late, what with the current fashion and pop-culture trends. But even discounting this, figures such as Blackbeard and Captain Kidd are household names. And surprisingly enough, villains that they were, these same names are looked on rather fondly. For whatever reason, deep down inside people generally harbor a special affection for pirates.

A love of pirates is what this site is all about. Sure, there's a love for the history, but mostly it's a love of the myth—the legends. Facts have their place, after all, but they should never be allowed to interfere with a good story. Peg legs and eye patches abound, and plank walking is a frequent activity. And while scurvy is a constant threat, it's more a colorful buzzword than a seriously debilitating condition involving spongy gums. Welcome to Bilgemunky.com.

Blackbeard's Realm (www.blackbeardsrealm.com).

Avast ye! Teach yourself whatever you want to know about the infamous Blackbeard, a terror of the seas.

Black Pearl Tales (www.blackpearltales.net).

Fan fiction.

Black Swan (www.angelfire.com/rpg2/blackswan/seabed.html).

Role-playing site where you can contribute to an ongoing pirate story.

Bloodthirsty Pirate Tales (www.pirate-tales.com).

Pirate tales in comic book form. Professional art by Richard Becker, known for his historical art for the cable TV channel, A&E.

Bonny's Buccaneers (www.bonnys-buccaneers.org.uk).

A collective of reenactors based in and around the southeast of England, West County, and Wales. The group's members have, cumulatively, 150 years of reenacting experience to their names.

Brethren of the Coast
(www.geocities.com/captcutlass/ index.html).

A good general-interest site for newcomers with sections on piracy in general, flags, weapons, ships, biographies, sea shanties, treasure, movies, ports of call, an art gallery, games, and a glossary.

Bring Me That Horizon
(www.geocities.com/emma_irlam/jacksparrow/jacksparrow.htm).

Tribute to Jack Sparrow/Johnny Depp.

Caboots
(www.caboots.com).

Sells leather boots of every kind, plus a great pirate costume.

Captain Blood's Cove
(www.geocities.com/cptblood_1999/ directory.html).

A good general-interest site with sections on tall ships, naval weaponry, and discipline at sea. An overview of the world of pirates.

Captain Jack's Pearls
(groups.yahoo.com/group/CaptainJackspearls).

"This group is dedicated to the shameless promotion of our own Captain Jack Sparrow and his crew of miscreants."

Captain Raven's Seadogs of the Eighteenth Century
(www.geocities.com/pirategrl666).

Dedicated to the golden age of piracy. General information, nautical terms and expressions, common misconceptions, etc. (Very difficult to read because of the white text against flame-colored wallpaper.)

Crew of the Dirty Rotten Oar (www.dirtyrottenoar.com).

Reenactors based in California, available for renaissance fairs and other events.

Costumer's Manifesto (www.costumes.org).

A superb, information-packed website about costumes, uniforms, and period clothing. The first place you should go before buying plunder wear.

Dark Tides (groups.msn.com/DarkTides/ridethedarktide.msnw).

Role-playing game. Read the site's code, its FAQs, and etiquette before signing your life away.

David Wenzel (www.davidwenzel.com).

A fantasy artist who offers prints of his artwork. In the "currently brewing" section, he's working on a book called *Skull & Crossbones: Tales from the Wicked Days of Piracy,* which is "an illustrated collection of narrative tales and swashbuckling trivia based on the real pirates of the Caribbean." When the book is out, let's hope he makes some prints of the cover available. The cover art is spectacular!

Dead Men Tell No Tales (www.deadmentellnotales.com)

Probably the most complete store of its kind, with more than two thousand pirate-related items in its inventory: a treasure chest of booty for anyone with a casual to a fanatic interest in pirates.

Pirate *Arrtist* Don Maitz (www.paravia.com/DonMaitz)

I was staring directly at a motley crew of forty thieves, who looked unlikely to give any quarter. Armed with flintlock pistols and rifles, swords, a swivel gun, cutlasses, and other fearsome weapons, these battle-hardened and bloodthirsty pirates on board this particular ship were ready to fight to the death!

Fortunately, it's not a real-world confrontation—it's a fantastic scene frozen in time, a snapshot of a pirate ship painted by artist Don Maitz, whose colorful painting visually greets visitors who had the good fortune to see "Swashbuckler: Romance of the

Eight-foot painting by Don Maitz of a pirate ship and
its motley crew, on display at the Mariners' Museum.

Pirate," an exhibit that ran for six months in 2006 at the Mariners'
Museum in Newport News, Virginia.

Meticulously painted, *Forty Thieves* sparks the imagination.
What, one wonders, is the story behind each of the forty pirates?
What is the history of the ship's captain, flamboyantly dressed in
red? What of the sharpshooter on the aft part of the ship, aiming his
flintlock rifle? And what about the young man who, as the battle is
underway, is lost in his own world, playing a violin? (Maitz himself
is in the painting five times in various guises, most notably behind the
gunner who is hoisting the Jolly Roger.)

A close-up of Maitz's pirate ship painting, on display at the Mariners' Museum.

The Maitz painting stole
the show, so to speak, at the
exhibit, by virtue of its size (40
x 84 inches) and visual impact.
Maitz's work of art does what
every work of art should do: It
transports the viewer into the
visual world depicted by the
artist, if only temporarily.

Which, in this case, is a *good* thing because here there be pirates. . . .

Forty Thieves is no longer available as a limited edition art print from Greenwich Workshop, but it is still available as a fold-out greeting card. (It was also used as a design for a puzzle, titled Pirates of the High Seas, and as a trading card.)

A close-up of Maitz's pirate ship painting, on display at the Mariners' Museum.

Maitz's other pirate art can be seen in a variety of publications and places: on the cover of *Pirates Magazine* (Autumn 2006), on the cover and interior pages of National Geographic's *Blackbeard: The Pirate King*, wall calendars from Ride-Mark Press, mugs and drinking glasses, jigsaw puzzles, greeting cards, art prints, and other products.

And if you're a fan of Seagram Corporation's Captain Morgan Spiced Rum, you've seen his work: He created the image of Captain Morgan, in various interpretations.

If you're able to see Maitz's pirate art in the original on exhibit at a gallery, convention, or museum show, you'll see (as I did) that his work is a visual treat. Here's a guy who loves painting, loves pirates, and combines both to stunning effect in his growing body of work that transports the viewer to the Golden Age of Pirates.

You can see Maitz's art at his official website at www.paravia.com, which he shares with his artist/writer wife, Janny Wurts.

Dress Like a Pirate (www.dresslikeapirate.com).

Jewelry, pirate costumes, hats, boots, and weapons. More expensive than Halloween costumes but less expensive than period clothing. In other words, an affordable line that's well worth a look.

Forget Me Not Factory (www.forgetmenotfactory.com).

Pirate toys and treasures, pirate t-shirts, pirate flags, pirate books, and pirate mugs.

Front Porch Classics (www.frontporchclassics.com).

Publishes a coffee-table game called "Dread Pirates." "Choose a ship, a port of call, and set sail in search of treasure. Be the first pirate to collect all types of jewels and land on Dread Island to become the most feared and powerful captain on the high seas."

Glaston Privateers (glastonpirates.guildporta.com).

Role-playing forum.

Gypsy Moon (www.gypsymoon.com).

For women only, this design studio/boutique was created by former dancer and costumer Candace Savage. This store features a high-end line of clothing "that is feminine, romantic, and timeless." In other words, it's not authentic pirate gear, but there are a lot of women in the pirate community who wear this clothing to pirate festivals and renaissance fairs.

International Talk Like a Pirate Day (www.talklikeapirate.com).

Celebrates September 19, which they have declared to be "Talk Like a Pirate" day. Of particular interest: a pirate talk generator, so you can type in text and have it translated: a good way to have a few phrases ready to use at the next pirate festival. According to its cofounder Cap'n Slappy (also known as Mark Summers), "We tell people to eat barbecue pork, drink lots of rum, and have a good time. It's the one holiday where you can dress like a pirate and walk down the street and it's okay that people yell 'Arrr!' at you from their cars."

Jolly Rogues (www.jollyrogues.com).

Home port, Massachusetts. A musical group whose members are also part of the Guild of Historical Interpreters. CDs available. Wonderful music that'll have you dancing a jig, but not a hempen one.

Jonathan White, mapmaker (www.indianbay.net)

Creates custom-made maps for use in nautical illustration, movie/TV props, gaming, publishing projects, etc. (His work can be seen on the cover and endpapers of this book.)

Lady Couture (www.ladycouture.com).

Custom-made clothing, but slim pickings so far: a $275 Jack Sparrow Leather Tricorne hat. Looks good, though, and let's hope there's more product up for sale. High quality goods here for that authentic touch.

Mallory and McCall (www.malloryandmccall.com).

Home base, southern California. A pirate band that frequently plays at pirate festivals and played at the premiere of the first Pirates of the Caribbean film. This website is packed to overflowing with information that's difficult to follow, and the layout is confusing.

Museum Replicas (www.museumreplicas.com).

This is a division of Atlanta Cutlery, which holds movie licenses for sword/battle ware replicas. (I've seen finished product from *The Lord of the Rings* line and it's first-rate.) Well worth your doubloons.

Musical Blades (www.musicalblades.com).

A musical group that plays primarily at renaissance fairs in the Midwest.

My Lady's Cutlass (www.myladyscutlass.com).

A musical duo that performs at public get-togethers. The duo (Jen Bradley and Kim Sobbe) merges "the essence of Celtic, French, and English folk music, featuring flutes, drums, psaltery, dulcimers, English bagpipes, and the resounding groan of the didgeridoo." CDs available. Related merchandise through www.cafepress.com.

Oak Island Revelations (www.oakislandrevelations.com).

A thorough look at the legend of buried treasure that purportedly belonged to Captain Kidd. Nothing's been found to date, but it didn't stop a lot of plunderers from trying!

The Open Seas (www.opensea.proboards7.com).
Bulletin board.

Passion for Pirates (www.home.att.net/~wnet3/passion).
Tribute to the Disney film *Pirates of the Caribbean*. A pretty thorough trivia section—more than most people would ever want to know. A link to information about the ride that inspired the film franchise. Fan fiction.

Pirate VI (www.pirate.vi).
Shirts, hats, books, and games. Small selection.

The Pirate Brethren (www.piratebrethren.com).
A reenacting group that goes by the name of Brethren of the Bay. Some members have more than two decades of experience as reenactors.

Pirate Documents (piratedocuments.com).
A very interesting site. Using a historically appropriate font and hand-processed paper, this company can produce authentic-looking period piece documents, such as a letter of marque with the wax seal. With informative sections about letters of marque, letters of reprisal, admiralty reports, instructions, articles of shipboard conduct, and more, this site is perfect for any pirate or privateer who wants to carry authentic-looking documentation. The best forgers in town!

The Pirate Empire (www.thepirateempire.com)
Pirate performers for pirate-related events. I had the good fortune of meeting Steve Dapcevich at the Blackbeard Festival in Hampton, Virginia, in June 2006. He simply stole the show appearing as a Jack Sparrow look-alike. With him was his fiancée, a slim, blonde-haired young woman also dressed in pirate-inspired clothing. Together, they look sensational and would add the right

atmosphere to any pirate-themed event. Trust me on this one: You couldn't do any better no matter where you look.

Pirate Event (www.piratevent.com).

General-interest pirate website with articles, gallery of pirate events pirate t-shirts, and other paraphernalia.

Pirate Pendants (piratependants.com).

Risedens Jewelers' custom pirate-themed jewelry.

Pirate Leatherworx (www.pyrate.org/plunder.html).

A line of made-to-order leather products like pouches, hats, belts, coin bags, etc.

Pirate Ring websites (www.geocities.com/p_irate_2000/ pirate.html)

A great place to go exploring on your own with more than one hundred websites.

Pirate Soul Museum (www.piratesoul.com)

The best pirate museum in the world. Bar none. This earns my highest recommendation.

Piratemerch.com (www.piratemerch.com).

Pirate merchandise. More along the lines of costuming, not authentic period clothing.

PirateMod (www.piratemod.com).

Alternative fashion with piratical attitude: t-shirts, sweatshirts, and hooded shirts. (For women, here are a few of their designs: "Prepared to be boarded," "Treasure Chest," and "Nice booty.")

Pirate's Brew Beer (www.piratesbrew.com).

How this company makes its beer, which is sold through retailers. (It's not available through the website.)

Pirates' Cave (www.pirates-cave.com).

Period clothing and weapons.

Pirates Code (bloodybugger.proboards85.com).

Bulletin board.

Pirate's Cove (www.thepirateking.com).

Rob Ossian's well-regarded general-interest website about all things pirate. Very well done! One of the best on the web! Huzzah!

Pirates Dinner Adventure (www.piratesdinneradventure.com).

In Buena Park, California, and Orlando. This sounds great to me: an authentically replicated eighteenth century Spanish galleon measuring forty-six feet long and eighteen feet wide, with 40-foot masts. It's anchored in a 300,000-gallon indoor lagoon with night sky lighting. Surrounding the lagoon is a six-sided showroom of six additional "ships" where the audience is seated. Voyagers on each of the six "ships" have their own fearless pirate "mascot" whom they cheer on as the adventure unfolds with a cast of a dozen actors, singers, and stunt performers engaging in a bounty of action-packed exploits, accompanied by cannon blasts, pyrotechnics, and a liberal dose of wit and wizardry. There's a preshow and a buffet, followed by a feast, the show itself, and dancing afterward. A full menu is posted online. Your mouth is guaranteed to water!

Pirates Hold (pirateshold.buccaneersoft.com).

A good website. "This site will try to contain the treasures of information, images, sources, and things related to pirates. It will concentrate on the historical aspects."

Pirates International (www.partners-international.org/pirates).

Sells various items with some of the proceeds going to help the less fortunate worldwide. "An organization dedicated to helping those in need throughout the world. All good pirates share their booty with their less fortunate shipmates, lest they be scuttled some day and in need themselves. So, 'Don't be snooty, just give up your booty.'"

Pirate's Lair (www.thepirateslair.com).

The place to buy antique naval chinaware and flatware.

Pirate's Life (apirateslife.cjb.net).

Role-playing game online.

Pirates Magazine (www.piratesmagazine.com).

This is the new entry in the field, edited and published by Kim Cross. Mainstream in appeal, it's issued on a quarterly basis. The first issue was launched in October 2006. $26 for four issues. Address: PO Box 26645, Gwynn Oak, MD 21207.

Pirates' Plunder (www.piratepeople.proboards15.com).

Message board for pirate role players. It used to be dedicated to the PC game, "Pirates of the Caribbean," but that's history.

Pirates' Plunder Mall (www.piratesplundermall.com).

In Newport, Oregon. An antique shop with more than eight thousand square feet of merchandise.

Privateers Scavenger Hunt (www.themeactorsgroup.com).

If you need pirates for your event, here's where you'll find a few sea dogs and buxom beauties based in South Lake Tahoe, California.

The Pirateses (geocities.com/thepirateses).

For younger readers, mostly. Has a fun section with quizzes using multiple choices to determine: What real pirate are you? What would you do in that pirate situation? And a Pirates of the Caribbean quiz.

Privateer Dragons of the Caribbean (www.privateerdragons.com).

Coverage of pirate fans at renaissance festivals. Includes some fun name generators. (Depending on whether I want an honorable or insulting name, I'm either Swashbuckler Stede Hornblower or Fobbing Milk-livered Flapdragon.)

POTC Fan Trips (www.potcfantrips.com).

I'm familiar with this company, Beyond Boundaries, a tour company that has hosted many well-received Harry Potter movie-themed trips. Now, they've turned their attention to nautical matters; or, more accurately, the *Pirates of the Caribbean* movies with trips tailored to California, Jamaica, the Bahamas, and St. Vincent. Well worth your time if you want to take a trip under the auspices of an experienced tour group.

Pyracy (www.pyracy.co.uk).

Pirate reenactors in the UK.

Pyracy Pub (pyracy.com).

A bulletin board and a photo gallery of people dressed up like pirates and pirate events (festivals). A good place to drop anchor and talk with like-minded pirate souls.

The Pyrates Way (www.pyratesway.com)

Like *Pirates Magazine,* this is a new venture. Its first issue is cover-dated autumn 2006, so it may be a quarterly. A general interest magazine, it's published by Steve Kimball. Four issues, $20. Address: The Pyrates Way, PO Box 1231, Bear, DE 19701.

Really Bad Eggs Custom Pirate Ships
(www.reallybadeggs.melbournefljaycees.org).

Constructs custom-made pirate ship floats.

Realms and Empires (www.realmsandempires.com).

A very complete store offering a full line of historical gifts and collectibles from select periods of history: medieval, Egyptian, Eastern, Roman, and of course, pirates. Product is sold on its eBay store. The pirate line emphasizes accessories, not clothing per se, though they do carry baseball hats, bandanas, etc.

Revered Order of Pirates and Rogues
(reveredorderofpiratesandrogues.com).

A club of pirate fans located in southeast Virginia. Looks like a fine bunch of swashbucklers that could use some more members.

Rillian and the Doxie Chicks (thedoxiechicks.3200bpm.com).

Musical group that performs for private functions, though they do support some renaissance fairs.

Rum Barrel (www.piratesoul.com/rumbarrel).

This colorful, pirate-themed restaurant in Key West is owned by Pat Croce. It's a great place to chow down after visiting Pat's most excellent museum, Pirate Soul.

Sea Rats (www.thatpirategame.com).

A pirate board game. "Send yer buddies down to Davy Jones' Locker. Capture 'the prize' an' build up a fleet o' ships! Brave her enemies te escape hostile fire—whatever it takes te be the last pirate afloat an' win the game!"

The Sheppey Pirates (www.sheppeypirates.org).

Reenactors. Lots of good links for detailed information on how they do what they do.

Skallywaggs (www.skallywaggs.com).

A stand-alone card game for 2 or 4 players. "Be the first to set sail by building a crew of rascally rogues before your opponents can complete their own collection of misfits. You'll need both luck and skill. But beware! This is Skallywaggs, and every pirate worth his parrot knows the tide is quick to turn."

The Scurvy Dogs (www.scurvydawgs.com).

A pirate comedy group and variety act based in Waukesha, Wisconsin. Will work for doubloons.

Sea Wolf Clothing and Accessories (www.seawolfonline.com).

Shirts, hats, and accessories.

Shiver My Timber
(www.antagonia.net/rogue/shiver/weblinks.php).

Role-playing. Also has some useful links for information on the seventeenth century, which helps in creating your character.

Silver Dragon Swords (www.silverdragonswords.com).

A wide selection of swords, armor, battle-axes, maces, flails, knives, throwing weapons. Disney fans will especially be interested in the Pirates of the Caribbean replica swords.

Silvermane (www.silvermane.com/pirates).

Carries merchandise from Roman to Renaissance times. Pirate products include tools of the trade (skeleton keys, ball and chain, padlock, compass, keys to the brig), leather accessories (belts, holsters, and baldrics), flags, flintlock pistols and powder horns, maps and games, and weapons (cutlasses).

Sparrow's Pearls (www.sparrowspearls.com).

Tribute to Jack Sparrow. Useful links.

Tales of Pirates and Buccaneers (www.panhistoria.com).

Registration required. Fan fiction: the Harry Potter universe, science fiction, vampires, monsters, etc. Pirates too, of course.

Tales of the Seven Seas (www.talesofthesevenseas.com).

A group of pirate reenactors available for public appearances. Bulletin board. Lots of excellent photos from cruises, reenactments, etc.

Tell No Tales (www.tellnotales.com).

A well-designed site, a tribute to Disney's pirate film franchise. Bulletin board. Information about the ride, the movie, fan-submitted stories and art, etc. A good place to start for any new fan of Disney's Pirates of the Caribbean movies and rides.

Thistles and Pirates (www.cindyvallar.com/pirates.html).

Webmaster, Cindy Vallar. A very well-written site with articles on pirates, excellent links, and book reviews.

Treasure Island (www.treasureisland.com).

There's no lack of shows to see in Vegas, but if you want a Vegas-style show with a pirate theme, check in at the Treasure Island hotel and check out its signature show, "Sirens of Treasure Island." No need to raid the treasure chest to see this show. It's free and runs four times a night at Sirens' Cove in front of the hotel on a re-created pirate ship. The show "begins with a seventeenth century clash between a group of beautiful, tempting sirens and a band of renegade pirates. With their mesmerizing and powerful song, the Sirens lure the pirates to their cove, stir up a tempest strong enough to sink a ship, and transform Sirens' Cove into a twenty-first century party for all to enjoy. From daring swordplay to high-diving acrobatics and eye-popping pyrotechnics, [this show] is packed with countless thrills." If you can't get to Vegas, check out the hotel's website to see a film clip of the show and high-resolution photos. NOTE: You can register to see the show live on the Sirens webcam nightly.

Triskelion Pirate Conspiracy (www.pirateconspiracy.com).

This group is based in San Antonio. They're working on a demo CD to help get bookings. If you're a local organization and need to have a few pirate songs belted out—"A Pirate's Life for Me!", "Drunken Sailor," "Black Dog's Curse," "Favorite Sins," etc.—drop them a line.

Triton's Fury (tritonsfury.com).

Home port, Battle Creek, Michigan. "We are a group of performers dedicated to entertaining the masses. We offer a wide range of entertainment from sea shanties to comedy skits, along with a traveling zoo of sorts made up of one crew member's myriad of amazing, exotic pets, including her pet dragon. We have performed in a number of states at renaissance fairs, pirate festivals, and private parties."

Under the Mystical Moon (www.underthemysticalmoon.com).
A fine line of leather goods, weapons, chain mail, etc.

Vigilante (www.vigilante.me.uk).
Chat room for pirate fans: one for adults, one for children.

4. No Quarter Given

From the No Quarter Given home page, "No Quarter Given is the clearinghouse for those interested in pirates, privateers, and nautical history."

Long before Disney's 2003 film *Pirates of the Caribbean* pushed pirates into the limelight, pirate fan-zines, websites, reenactments, musical groups, and pirate festivals had been enjoying a resurgence of interest in a big way. Disney's film, however, pushed it over the top. The salutary effect of Disney's newest film franchise has been seen across the board for pirate vendors. As Jon Biggs, co-owner of costumezone.com, explains, it's "high tide," not only for pirate costumes, but for all things piratical.

Among pirate fandom, one website has reigned supreme: It's noquartergiven.net. The watering hole for pirate fans worldwide, this site is simply the best. Christine Markel Lampe and her husband Michael Lampe probably know everything there is to know about pirates. Here's an abbreviated list of what's on their website—all proof positive that if you're setting sail on the web for information, this is an essential port of call.

No Quarter Given Magazine

Published six times a year ($12 if sent by bulk mail, $17 by first class mail), this magazine "will bring you generously illustrated articles on the history, lore, romance, and sheer adventure of being a pirate or privateer." It focuses squarely on the seventeenth to early eighteenth century, when piracy flourished. Required reading for anyone seriously interested in pirates, its first issue was published in 1994. Annual compilations of back issues are available by year, which is a good way to start a reference library, of course. Back issues, however, are available if you want to "try before you buy" a year's worth.

L.O.R.E. Workshops and Classes

In conjunction with the Crossroads Group, No Quarter Given (NQG) organizes workshops and classes for aspiring pirates billed as the Loyal Order of Reenactment Enthusiasts (L.O.R.E.). A lot of ground is covered in one short weekend: pirate history and culture, pirate costuming, advanced black powder, swordplay, introduction to cannons, pirate persona development, beginning black powder, dockside tavern songs, talk like a pirate, games pirates played, and historic rogues meet at the tavern.

On the home page, links are provided to navigate to the various major categories of information:

Events

This lists upcoming events in chronological order, with web links for more information. The list is a moving document; it is updated on a regular basis.

Pirate and Privateer Crews

This is a regional listing of pirate crews, both well-established and new crews looking to add more hands aboard. This page includes pointers on starting your own crew if you're new to the "sweet trade."

Merchants and Smugglers

The definitive list of places to go to buy pirate-related or pirate-inspired products. In cases where NQG has personal knowledge of

the company, it awards three skulls, which denotes "merchants &
smugglers with whom we have trafficked, and whose merchandise
we can heartily recommend." It cautions that "if a merchant doesn't
have the three skulls rating, it doesn't necessarily mean they aren't
to be trusted or that they sell inferior goods; it just means we don't
have firsthand knowledge of them."

The categories covered include: books, music, maps, movies,
cannons, large guns, coins, costuming, period clothing, footwear,
living history suppliers, nautical suppliers, pirate specialists, periodicals, tents/pavilions, treasure and jewelry, and weapons.

Books

An exhaustive list of recommended books: beginning buccaneering, nonfiction, advanced general buccaneering, specialized
nonfiction, biographies, nautical and military information, songs
and sea chanteys, classic pirate fiction, pirate nonfiction for children, and pirate fiction for children.

Also provided are recommended merchants who specialize in
pirate books, with a specialist's breadth of knowledge that general
booksellers lack.

Rogues Gallery

A photo gallery of some of the contributors to *NQG* magazine
and some of the characters they know who attend pirate festivals.
Not surprisingly, you'll find some great costumes on display here.
These folks take their pirating v-e-r-y seriously.

Movie Guide

A listing of pirate movies, release dates, stars, and subject matter. A good place to start if you want to know what's been released.
Did you know, for instances, that there are three Peter Pan movies,
not including sequels?

Tall Ships

Write-ups and links on tall ships on which the NQG crew has sailed. Photos of each ship, information about its lineage, etc. Hey, whatever floats your boat, right?

Ports o' Call on the Internet

A treasure trove of resources. I can't imagine they've missed anything here.

1. Buccaneers of old: piracy in general, privateering and letters of marque, individual pirates, pirate study lessons for young 'uns and not-so-young 'uns, modern piracy, and pirate sites (non-English).

2. Salamagundi: books, plays, and poems; pirate movies; pirate museums, groups, festivals, and shows; musical pirates and salty songs with a roguish touch; swashbuckling artists and illustrated pirate tales; games, puzzles, jokes, and frivolous activities; buccaneering food and drink; and miscellaneous piratical endeavors.

3. Nautical sites and maritime museums: general maritime sites, celebrating voyages of old, maritime museums, maritime reenactment groups, sea songs, and shanties.

4. Tall ships

5. Living history

6. Costuming and outfitting for pirates

7. Miscellaneous interesting sites

5. DISNEY RESOURCES

The official website (www.disney.com) takes you to any place in the Disney universe. Pirate fans should visit "Disney Destinations" to explore Disneyland Resort, Walt Disney World, and the Disney Cruise Line.

World Premiere of the Films

Disneyland Resort is where the world premieres of *The Curse of the Black Pearl* and *Dead Man's Chest* were held, with the traditional red carpet roll-out. At this writing, no announcement has been made regarding the world premiere of *At World's End,* but if Disney follows suit, the red carpet will roll out in Disneyland Resort and fans can catch a glimpse of their favorite stars as they walk the red carpet.

Tickets for the world premiere itself are not available to the public. Like other premieres, you either have to be a Very Important Person (by Hollywood standards) or know somebody who can get you a ticket.

Disneyland Resort

Although there's lots of licensed film-related *Pirates of the Caribbean* product available at the official Disney website and online through other vendors, exclusive merchandise is available at the theme parks. After getting off the

A pin design from Disney's extensive *Pirates of the Caribbean* pin collection.

Pirates of the Caribbean ride, check out its gift shop, which will have a range of product from children to adults.

Walt Disney World

In the Magic Kingdom: Go to the gift shop after you get off the Pirates of the Caribbean ride. You could spend a lot of time and money here, since the selection is extensive. I can't imagine being a fan of the movies and leaving empty-handed. (I picked up an ornate but affordable picture frame and an 18-inch sculpted figurine of Captain Jack Sparrow.)

In the Disney-MGM Studios

Go to Sid Cahuenga's One-of-a-Kind Antiques and Curios. Curiously, this is not listed (though it is depicted) on the official map given out as you enter the park. Located to your immediate left as you pass through the entrance, it's a treasure trove of signed memorabilia—photos, books, posters, and movie stills. (I got a

Sid Cahuenga's One-of-a-Kind Antiques and Curios.

matted photo of Johnny Depp as Captain Jack Sparrow for $25. There was also for sale a signed photo by him for $450—I passed on it.)

The second place to go is the Animation Courtyard at Disney-MGM Studios, which offers a $150 replica of *The Black Pearl*; an open edition, it's made of resin and is exquisitely detailed.

Memberships to the Walt Disney Collectors Society are available here through their authorized dealers or online

The Pirates of the Caribbean sign outside the ride itself at Walt Disney World Resort in Orlando, Florida.

for $50. This allows you to get advance notice on exclusive sculpture, including the new pirate line, available only to Collectors Society members. (For enrollment or other information, see waltdisneyclassicscollection.com).

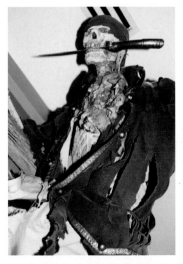

A skeletal pirate with dagger in teeth on display at the World of Disney retail store.

Finally, for those who want to immerse themselves in a unique experience, there's the "Pirates of the Caribbean: Adventure on the 7 Seas Lagoon (May 22–25, 2007, at Disney's Contemporary Resort at Walt Disney World). Several packages are available ranging from $199 to $2350. For specifics, go to disneygallery.com and click on the appropriate link under Walt Disney World Resort.

Downtown Disney

Go to the flagship store, World of Disney, located on the east side of Disney Marketplace, which is located off Buena Vista Drive east of Typhoon Lagoon. In addition to every conceivable Disney product at prices that range from pocket change to serious bucks, the extensive product line of pirate-related merchandise could fill a Spanish galleon.

For an interactive adventure, check out DisneyQuest, which offers "Pirates of the Caribbean: Battle for Buccaneer Gold. Put on your headpiece to inhabit a world booming with swashbuckling action. Steer your ship, fire cannons at marauding buccaneers, and race for the gold!"

The Official Fan Site

To keep on top of what's available, go to keepthecode.com, which is the official fan site for Disney's *Pirates of the Caribbean* movies. The site is updated regularly and has a lot of information: news, key events, the films, a messageboard, etc. Well worth your time.

A skeletal ship's captain with spyglass and blunderbuss on display at the World of Disney retail store.

A Disney collectible, a figurine of "Helmsman Pirate" from the Walt Disney Classics Collection.

Pirate Sculpture

These pieces, from the Walt Disney Classics Collection, are offered for sale at the theme parks but not through their retail network. The pieces in this collection include: "Helmsman Pirate" (a skeletal figure at the helm), $299; "Captain of *The Wicked Wench*" (a pirate looking over the side of a ship), $250; and "We Wants the Redhead!" (a pair featuring the comely redhead from the Pirates ride and a pirate brandishing a whip), $299.

A pirate with parrot sits amidst his booty in an elaborate display at the World of Disney retail store.

Acknowledgments

What a cruise this book has been! Will the following brethren of the coast please step up on the poop deck and take their well-deserved bows?

To the crew of the good ship Hampton Roads Publishing, who saw fit to launch another "ship" of mine so to speak. All the good folks there had a hand in this book, and because there are too many to name individually, you all know who you are, so take a bow. But I would be remiss if I didn't thank Bob, Jack, Tania, and Jane, who got this ship out of dry dock and set it on its steady course.

To the female members of the crew, who brought me all sorts of good luck: Britton McDaniel and, of course, my wife Mary.

Britton, once again, took time out of her busy schedule to work on this book, providing a colorful and eye-catching portrait of a pirate captain at sea.

To cartographer Jonathan White, whose map more than fits the bill.

To the fine folks at the Mariners' Museum, who allowed me to fire at will—i.e., take all the photos I needed.

And, finally, to "Long John" Tim Kirk, whom I'm privileged to call a friend. Once again, Tim, you've dropped more important work to aid me on mine, for which I am indebted. The introduction, the pen-and-ink illustrations, the color piece of the treasure chest, and all the behind-the-scenes advice about pirates—you certainly helped this landlubber!

Thank you, one and all.

Arr! Join the Sweet Trade!

art by Britton McDaniel

THE CREW:
ABOUT THE AUTHOR AND ILLUSTRATORS

Britton McDaniel, George Beahm, and Tim Kirk at a
book signing at Whimsic Alley in Santa Monica, California.

Author **George Beahm** rejuvenated the literary companion book format with the 1989 publication of *The Stephen King Companion*. He has published more than two dozen nonfiction books, including titles on Michael Jordan, Stephen King, Anne Rice, Patricia Cornwell, C. S. Lewis, J. R. R. Tolkien, J. K. Rowling, and Philip Pullman. A book industry expert who has worked as a self-publisher, regional publisher, author, marketing director, book designer, book packager, and marketing consultant, Beahm lives with his wife Mary in Williamsburg. His website is www.georgebeahm.com.

Artist **Britton McDaniel** is a graduate of Virginia Commonwealth University, with a bachelor of arts in communication, arts, and design, with a concentration in illustration. She has also attended the Illustration Academy, where she worked closely with top US illustrators. A freelance artist, she lives in Mechanicsville, Virginia. Her recent credits include interior art for a book about Harry Potter, *Fact, Fiction, and Folklore in Harry Potter's World,* and a cover design for *The Truth about Medium.* Her website is www.BrittonMcDaniel.com.

Artist **Tim Kirk** is a design director for Kirk Design, which draws on his vast experience in conceptualization, content creation, and art direction at Walt Disney Imagineering, where he worked for twenty-two years. Among his many credits at Disney, Kirk was the overall senior designer for Tokyo DisneySea, a three billion dollar theme park. He also played a key role in conceptualizing the popular Disney MGM Studio Tour Park in the Walt Disney World Resort. A five-time Hugo award winner for best art in the fantasy and science fiction field, Kirk has illustrated fanzines, calendars, limited edition books, and trade books for numerous publishers, including Ballantine Books, which issued his Tolkien illustrations, done for his master's degree in illustration, as the 1975 *Tolkien Calendar.* A former artist for both Hallmark Cards and Current, Kirk has designed greeting cards, jigsaw puzzles, wrapping paper, stationery, and books. In June 2004, one of Kirk Design's projects made its debut: The Science Fiction Museum and Hall of Fame in Seattle, Washington. Kirk Design's website is www.kirkdesigninc.com.

SEA FEVER

by John Masefield

I must go down to the seas again, to the lonely sea and
the sky,
And all I ask is a tall ship and a star to steer her by,
And the wheel's kick and the wind's song and the white
sail's shaking,
And a gray mist on the sea's face, and a gray dawn
breaking.

I must go down to the seas again, for the call of the
running tide
Is a wild call and a clear call that may not be denied;
And all I ask is a windy day with the white clouds flying,
And the flung spray and the blown spume, and the sea
gulls crying.

I must go down to the seas again, to the vagrant gypsy life,
To the gull's way and the whale's way, where the wind's
like a whetted knife;
And all I ask is a merry yarn from a laughing fellow rover,
And quiet sleep and a sweet dream when the long
tricks over.

FAREWELL!

HAMPTON ROADS PUBLISHING COMPANY
publishes books on a variety of subjects,
including metaphysics, spirituality,
health, visionary fiction, and other related topics.

For a copy of our latest trade catalog,
call toll-free, 800-766-8009,
or send your name and address to:

HAMPTON ROADS PUBLISHING COMPANY, INC.
1125 STONEY RIDGE ROAD • CHARLOTTESVILLE, VA 22902
E-mail: hrpc@hrpub.com • Internet: www.hrpub.com